JOB ARCHITECTURE

BEN ZWEIG

JOB ARCHITECTURE

BUILDING A LANGUAGE FOR WORKFORCE INTELLIGENCE

Copyright © 2026 by John Wiley & Sons, Inc. All rights reserved, including rights for text and data mining and training of artificial intelligence technologies or similar technologies.

Published by John Wiley & Sons, Inc., Hoboken, New Jersey.

No part of this publication may be reproduced, stored in a retrieval system, or transmitted in any form or by any means, electronic, mechanical, photocopying, recording, scanning, or otherwise, except as permitted under Section 107 or 108 of the 1976 United States Copyright Act, without either the prior written permission of the Publisher, or authorization through payment of the appropriate per-copy fee to the Copyright Clearance Center, Inc., 222 Rosewood Drive, Danvers, MA 01923, (978) 750-8400, fax (978) 750-4470, or on the web at www.copyright.com. Requests to the Publisher for permission should be addressed to the Permissions Department, John Wiley & Sons, Inc., 111 River Street, Hoboken, NJ 07030, (201) 748-6011, fax (201) 748-6008, or online at http://www.wiley.com/go/permission.

The manufacturer's authorized representative according to the EU General Product Safety Regulation is Wiley-VCH GmbH, Boschstr. 12, 69469 Weinheim, Germany, e-mail: Product_Safety@wiley.com.

Trademarks: Wiley and the Wiley logo are trademarks or registered trademarks of John Wiley & Sons, Inc. and/or its affiliates in the United States and other countries and may not be used without written permission. All other trademarks are the property of their respective owners. John Wiley & Sons, Inc. is not associated with any product or vendor mentioned in this book.

Limit of Liability/Disclaimer of Warranty: While the publisher and the authors have used their best efforts in preparing this work, including a review of the content of the work, neither the publisher nor the authors make any representations or warranties with respect to the accuracy or completeness of the contents of this work and specifically disclaim all warranties, including without limitation any implied warranties of merchantability or fitness for a particular purpose. No warranty may be created or extended by sales representatives, written sales materials or promotional statements for this work. The fact that an organization, website, or product is referred to in this work as a citation and/or potential source of further information does not mean that the publisher and authors endorse the information or services the organization, website, or product may provide or recommendations it may make. This work is sold with the understanding that the publisher is not engaged in rendering professional services. The advice and strategies contained herein may not be suitable for your situation. You should consult with a specialist where appropriate. Further, readers should be aware that websites listed in this work may have changed or disappeared between when this work was written and when it is read. Neither the publisher nor authors shall be liable for any loss of profit or any other commercial damages, including but not limited to special, incidental, consequential, or other damages.

For general information on our other products and services or for technical support, please contact our Customer Care Department within the United States at (800) 762-2974, outside the United States at (317) 572-3993 or fax (317) 572-4002.

Wiley also publishes its books in a variety of electronic formats. Some content that appears in print may not be available in electronic formats. For more information about Wiley products, visit our web site at www.wiley.com.

Library of Congress Cataloging-in-Publication Data is Available:

ISBN 978-1-394-36906-5 (Cloth)
ISBN 978-1-394-36907-2 (ePub)
ISBN 978-1-394-36908-9 (ePDF)

Cover Design: Wiley
Author Photo: Courtesy of the Author

SKY10131526_111725

*To the scientists advancing the way we understand work,
and to the future workers who will inherit
the world they help shape*

Contents

Foreword		ix
	Introduction: Wasting Our Most Precious Resource	1
Part I	**The Theory of Taxonomies**	**15**
Chapter 1	The Architecture of Work	17
Chapter 2	Why Work Gets Organized into Jobs	29
Chapter 3	How Jobs Transform	47
Chapter 4	Technologies and Transformation	59
Part II	**How to Build Taxonomies**	**79**
Chapter 5	The Fundamentals of Building a Taxonomy	81
Chapter 6	Creating a Complete Workforce Taxonomy	103

| Chapter 7 | The Right Way to Construct Taxonomies | 115 |

| **Part III** | **Using Taxonomies** | **129** |

Chapter 8	How Taxonomies Support Employees and Job Seekers	131
Chapter 9	How Taxonomies Can Help Investors	141
Chapter 10	How Taxonomies Enable Organizational Success	159
Conclusion:	*Putting Job Architecture to Work—Everywhere*	173

Notes	179
Acknowledgments	183
About the Author	185
Index	187

Foreword

BEN ZWEIG POINTS out in this intriguing book that a common language of work, or "job architecture" as Ben calls it—if it existed—could empower organizations, workers, leaders, policymakers, and others to make better decisions about talent, organizations, and the work relationship. As work becomes more fluid, boundaryless, and perpetually changing, such empowerment is increasingly needed to address social and organizational challenges such as work automation, fractional work, AI, work flexibility, equity, globalization, and a host of other headline issues.

Yet progress toward such a universal language of work has been glacially slow.

In my 40 years of research, consulting, coaching, and writing, working with hundreds of HR leaders and organizations globally, I've observed an overlooked and untapped opportunity to enhance work-related decisions. It lies dormant in what is traditionally known as job analysis. The term conjures up one of the most clerical of HR department duties, the administration of job descriptions—those lists of tasks, responsibilities, qualifications, and performance indicators—all summarized in a job title. Best practices suggest this should be a careful process, including research on jobs inside and outside the organization, interviews with workers and their managers, shadowing workers on the job, and surveys of how employees spend their time at work. All of this is to be done annually, or even more frequently if work is fast-changing (and what work isn't these days?). Yet such careful work is costly and time consuming, and demonstrates no immediate ROI, so most job descriptions are vague, inaccurate, and/or outdated.

That's dangerous, because those job descriptions are the basis for most HR activities (pay, development, hiring, performance management, etc.). When translated to job postings and hiring specifications, they are the first representation of the work that potential candidates encounter. When the job descriptions are vague or outdated or reflect the perspective of a single organization, they fail to reach their potential to serve as an essential building block for a common language of work.

Ben Zweig offers some hope in this book, based on his decades of experience as a data scientist at IBM and now as the CEO of Revelio Labs, an HR analytics company that is applying state-of-the-art statistical analysis, machine learning, AI, and large language models, to gather and synthesize information from job postings, online candidate profiles, and other public sources. I've long been a fan of this work, and Ben and I have a regular cadence of conversations about its implications. Revelio Labs uses its insights to help investors better understand which companies are losing key talent (such as AI engineers), and which companies are finding and attracting that talent. A vital requirement for such analysis is getting the work classification correct and consistent, so that comparisons can be made across different organizations.

Ben and I have regular conversations about the evolution of work and jobs. I've watched Ben grow into a thoughtful and rigorous authority on the evolution and future of work. His ideas are grounded in data, informed by practice, and forward-looking. This book represents a peek into how the next generation of thought leaders will approach work.

One reason I became intrigued Ben and his team's work was when he shared an example: Company A was posting a job with one label (say, AI Engineer), while Company B posted a job with the same work activities but a different label (say, AI Architect). Because the most talented applicants had experience using the first label, the first company got a lot more applicants than the second one. Language matters, and the Revelio Labs analysis revealed why.

As HR and workforce analytics are increasingly driven by technologies like AI and LLMs, Ben argues that we need no longer tolerate the Tower of Babel that characterizes the language of work. He describes an aspirational future where "job architecture" is more consistent, evidence-based, and fluidly adaptable using sophisticated data and analysis. My research suggests that foundational concepts may need to be rethought, such as "work without jobs." The emerging language of work will be pivotal to such an evolution. If we don't clarify the architecture of work, we risk carrying old inefficiencies into a new digital era.

My own work has shown how deconstructing jobs, job holders, and job qualifications into their components (such as tasks, capabilities, skills, and learning) can help leaders better understand and design work in a fluid and fast-changing environment. Ben's approach is different but complementary. He shows the promise of deep and comprehensive labor market data, to reveal how actual leaders, workers, and job seekers combine these components and label them as job descriptions. His analysis can reveal the architecture of work that underlies the jobs.

One of the hottest topics in HR right now is the notion of skill-based approaches to work, employment, and job/organization design, including emerging HR technologies, consulting approaches, and strategic talent planning tools/processes. The popular notion is that we must shift from job-based to skill-based work processes in areas such as recruitment, selection, learning, remuneration, careers, and AI integration. While I applaud the instinct to consider work at a more molecular level, "skills" are only one of many such molecular elements. We are in dire need of frameworks that consider the full array of such elements, and how they are being organized into work architecture, through the actual decisions of workers, organizations, job seekers, and others, operating in actual labor markets. As organizations grapple with rapid change, having a clear, thoughtful framework for work architecture is more important than ever.

Thus, this book appears at a critical moment. We have the opportunity and the necessity to rethink how work elements such as skills, tasks, capabilities, and jobs relate to each other, to our work systems, to the decisions of workers/leaders/policymakers, and ultimately to the global labor market systems. Vague, incomplete, or incorrect work language contributes to needless inefficiency, cost, bias, inequity, and wasted resources. Work is far too important to tolerate such a situation.

This book will inspire reflection and debate, a worthy aspiration. It offers an important evidence-based perspective that deserves a prominent place in the evolution of a new understanding of work and labor markets.

Dr. John Boudreau
Senior Research Scientist and Emeritus Professor
Center for Effective Organizations
University of Southern California

Introduction: Wasting Our Most Precious Resource

My first job after graduating with my PhD in economics was at IBM in 2015. I had considered pursuing a path that was more typical for people with my background—finance or consulting—but I thought that, as an economist, I should see how goods and services get made in the real world.

I was hired as a data scientist in IBM's Chief Analytics Office. This team essentially served as an internal consulting team, in that we were "hired" by other IBM teams to help them solve problems or answer questions using data. The team supported things like risk modeling, sales channel optimization, marketing analytics, and revenue forecasting.

I had a labor economics background, so I was going to work specifically on IBM's *people* analytics, in which we used data about the internal workforce to model and analyze employee trends. I was excited to join this team because IBM had a reputation as a leader in the relatively new field of people analytics.

On my first day of the job, the director of the Chief Analytics Office pulled me into his office and told me something that would change the course of my career.

He sat me down and told me why the stakes of this team's work were so high. He said that if you took the entire IBM budget and pulled out the total amount of money spent on people, this would make up about two-thirds of the company budget. Yet, despite employees being the overwhelming majority of costs, the company understood little about how this resource—its people—were being used.

It was our job to understand this resource better. We were a team of seven people, but with our analyses, we could alter the course of this generations-old company. We could help it make smarter, better decisions about its workforce, improving the bottom line while also improving the well-being of its employees.

I left that first meeting with my new boss feeling energized and inspired to get to work. Even though I had a PhD in labor economics, I never considered how little we understood the workforce and how little we were optimizing the most important resource in a company.

I quickly got access to IBM's entire HR database and tried to get a handle on it as soon as I could. The rest of my team was already working on an employee retention project, looking at the different factors that kept people working for the company and offering recommendations on how to reduce turnover.

I worked long hours, late into the night, testing out different models and running different analyses, but I got up every morning full of energy and excited to go to work to see what we would create that day.

The retention project I joined went over well with IBM's leadership. We offered clear recommendations on how to reduce turnover, centering on a retention bonus to top performers, which would incentivize longevity. The recommendation to incentivize longevity was based on the analysis of small groups of employees who would remain at the company for longer, the more they were paid. From this finding, we determined that offering increased compensation based on tenure would significantly enhance employee retention.

Throughout this project, I began to realize that there were some issues with the way we were collecting data and creating our analyses. Because we had access to internal data only, we could compare salaries—and, therefore, the effect of higher payment on retention—just with internal IBM employees. That was obviously a limiting factor for our data, because people never compare themselves just to their colleagues. Employees, especially high-performing ones, have an entire job market out there to find another job. What was important was not the opportunities within IBM but the opportunities drawing them to other companies.

Unfortunately, though, there would have been no way to compare salaries to other jobs outside the company because we had no real idea what employees were doing at those other jobs. Sure, the titles may have been the same, but was one associate manager at a competitor the same as an associate manager at IBM? There was no way to know, and there was no way to compare salaries and determine the appropriate influence on retention.

Despite these concerns with data, the leadership team was happy with our results, and we continued our work.

From Success to Frustration

Next, the IBM leadership wanted me and my team to support the Consulting Division. They wanted to project demand for company services, in part to help hire the right people for future client projects.

Through our analysis, we were able to model what we felt would be in-demand trends, based on what requests were being made from inside the company. The company had an internal team to help staff consulting projects, and the partners would request certain positions based on what work they were securing from clients. We took a look at all those requests and made some recommendations on where we saw demand for hiring.

Our results looked promising and exciting, but once we dug into them, we saw a big problem: They did not make any sense at all.

The output from our project was a set of occupations that showed the highest in-demand jobs at the top of the list and the least in-demand jobs at the bottom. But we received very conflicting results. For example, we had the job title "SAP Implementation Consultant" at the top. Based on our analysis, this job should have been the most in-demand position out there, indicating that potential clients likely would need support in SAP implementation in the coming months and years. (SAP, if you aren't familiar, is basically a comprehensive business management software.)

However, we also saw that SAP implementation specialist was at the absolute bottom of the list, meaning it was in the least demand. Yet if you looked deeper at the job specifications and requirements of these two positions, they were almost exactly the same. Functionally, they were no different. It was just that some teams referred to them as SAP implementation consultant and some used a slightly different term, SAP implementation specialist.

How could these similar occupations have such dramatically different demands? One part of our analysis was telling us to invest heavily in SAP consultancy because potential clients had a high interest in those implementations. But another part was saying the exact opposite: There was no demand at all for that kind of work, so don't bother with it.

We were dealing with an issue as old as the practice of data analysis: Garbage in, garbage out.

Through this project, I realized something: The way we think about jobs these days is a complete mess. Most companies are not good at defining jobs, and even if they were, it would not matter because there is no standard way to define jobs across companies and industries. Just like with the retention project, there was no way to understand if one job at one company was materially similar to a job with the same title at another. The jobs are labeled the same, but are they actually the same?

If we do not have good data on the workforce—if *no one* has good data—then we cannot help leaders make better decisions about their employees. We will remain in the dark, with the majority of our business expenses going to a resource that we cannot fundamentally understand. What's worse, that resource is not something material; the resource is human beings with livelihoods.

Without better data, organized and categorized in an effective way, we cannot help companies do better and we cannot improve the material well-being of employees. We are left flying blind.

Are We Making the Right Decisions?

My story is representative of many people now working in HR across industries. They are tasked with making decisions about our economy's most important resource—human labor—without being equipped with what they need to make those decisions effectively.

I wanted to start this book with my story to show the very real stakes when companies do not use good data to make decisions about human resources and labor within their workforce and across industries. Many companies are suffering the way my old employer did: They think they are making the right choices, but there is no way to know for certain.

Human capital is often the largest expense in any company, even as most companies have the least amount of reliable information about their workforce. Company leaders are making their biggest decisions with the least amount of information.

How did we get to the point where the thing that matters most to most companies—their employees—operates at the highest level of inefficiency? To answer this question, first I need to share a little bit about basic economic theory.

Capital and Labor Markets: The Basics

To simplify, everything in our economy—from the food we eat, the cars we drive, the houses we live in, the computers we work on, the entertainment we consume—are the product of two fundamental resources: capital and labor.

Capital consists of the physical things that help us produce what we need to produce: the big manufacturing plants and construction equipment all the way down to the laptops we use to send our work emails and write our memos. *Labor* is the work of humans using that capital to create goods and services. Anything our economy produces is the result of those two inputs. Businesses take labor and capital and put them together to create the things we want and need.

One important thing to know about the differences between capital and labor is that the size of each is significantly different. Turns out, my boss's assessment of the IBM workforce is more or less true across our economy. I won't get into the math, but, basically, economists have determined that the labor markets are about twice the size of the capital markets. Put another way, capital makes up about one-third of the economy whereas labor makes up about two-thirds.

Currently, we have a very scientific and very sophisticated way to allocate capital in this economy: our financial markets. The financial markets have become very scientific and very efficient at allocating capital. If you've visited Wall Street in the past several decades, you don't see people yelling at each other to trade stocks. Instead, what you'll see is actually quite boring: not much happening. Most people on Wall Street don't work on the stock exchange anymore. Instead, they're in offices, sitting behind computers, analyzing countless data points every day.

Unfortunately, that level of scientific rigor does not exist for labor markets. This is especially problematic because, by some estimates, organizations spend from 50 to 85% of their expenses on employee salaries and benefits. Employees alone typically account for more than half of an organization's operating budget.[1]

Despite the amount of money companies spend on talent, managing human capital remains challenging. Physical capital is relatively easy to move around, as a truck doesn't complain when it's shipped across state lines. But people might have some feelings about moving across the world just because their employer thinks their skills are needed in a different market.

The human capital market needs to take into account employee and employer preferences, and this important "matching" component makes it much harder to create efficiency within the market. Finding a good employer is like finding a spouse. It doesn't happen overnight. You have to kiss a lot of frogs until you find your Prince or Princess Charming. This is true for both employee and employer, and that process can drain a lot of resources. Companies might spend up to $20,000 just to hire one employee.[2] It's painful for a company if that hire does not work out.

We do not have to operate in this way. We can transform HR—and human capital generally—to be more data-driven, to be more responsive, and, most important, to be more efficient. We can improve the process so that we have to kiss fewer frogs before the perfect employee finds the perfect employer. We can also look to the future and plan better for how employees are used. With better data—and, most important, better categorization of that data—we can transform the labor markets to become better structured.

How can I be so confident about this? Because it's already happened before for capital markets. We did not start out with the level of efficiency that we see now. In fact, for most of human history, our capital markets operated quite inefficiently.

From Pigeons to Bloomberg Terminals

If we want to live in a productive and efficient society, we have to make sure that our two main resources—capital and labor—are allocated well. If they aren't, good businesses aren't getting the capital they need to grow. Potential employees aren't being hired to do jobs that are needed.

The history of the US financial markets starts soon after the Revolutionary War. A group of merchants and traders came together in May 1792 outside of a building at 68 Wall Street, signing what's known as the Buttonwood Agreement, named for the tree they would usually meet under, in secret, to try to establish rules of trade.[3]

Prior to this agreement, brokers had to work through auctioneers for the sale of commodities like wheat or tobacco. The Buttonwood Agreement essentially cut out the middleman, eliminating the need to go through auctioneers as intermediaries and allowing brokers to deal directly with each other or on behalf of clients. This was the birth of what we now know as the New York Stock Exchange. But in those early days, the stock market was still relatively inefficient. The brokers had bypassed the auctioneers, but they still did not have good information about the markets that could lead to a good distribution of capital. Anyone with insights on some kind of major development that no one else had could exploit that information advantage for a huge gain.

One legend tells the story of how Nathan Rothschild, using carrier pigeons, learned of Napoleon's defeat at Waterloo and was able to purchase British government bonds before anyone else had learned of the battle's outcome. Through that investment he built his fortune.[4]

Rothschild was able to exploit the weakness in the market for his own gain, which highlights how, without good information, capital markets could not function at their highest levels of efficiency. For a while, the *Wall Street Journal* was the only source of information for Wall Street traders, and the advice within those papers was not much better than guess or conjecture. Once prices for the sale of stocks and other financial products were made public and more accessible, smarter decision-making and analysis resulted.

The government also got involved in working with companies to make the markets function more efficiently. The Securities and Exchange Commission began to regulate disclosure for companies, requiring them all to share information about their operations in the same standardized ways. We now have armies of accountants and auditors to make sure disclosed information adheres to generally accepted accounting principles. While this may be a headache for companies around audit time, this process helps companies operate in a standardized way, allowing financial institutions to compare and contrast their operations and direct capital to where it is needed.

Thanks to this wealth of data that's easily categorized, much smarter decision making can be enabled that helps to allocate capital more effectively. If a company needs a loan or wants venture capital to help it grow, it can tap into a robust market of investors to access that capital.

Investors also have tools at their disposal to understand which companies represent a solid investment and which might be more risky. Almost every person on Wall Street has their own Bloomberg Terminal, which brings together data points on the financial markets, standardized and categorized across companies and industries. If you go into a finance firm, you'll see that everyone has two screens: the screen in front of them where they do their "day job." Right next to that screen is the Bloomberg Terminal that contains any and all information about the financial markets they could ever want. That wealth of information augments their day-to-day tasks.

The data flowing through the Bloomberg Terminals, unfortunately, can tell traders next to nothing about human capital, even though it is the primary input to almost all companies these days. The companies themselves have very little information that is reliable and standardized to help support their own operations. While Wall Street traders are no longer flying blind when it comes to their investment decisions, most executives and HR professionals are when it comes to the human decisions that matter most.

Luckily, a new direction and new approach to human capital management could be available and accessible to us all. We do not need to be flying blind.

Taxonomies Will Change How We Think About Work

The fundamental building block we need to analyze data properly is readily available to us, with a little work: taxonomies.

Taxonomy is a fancy way of saying we place things into categories. Taxonomies are fundamental to our lives. For instance, we teach our babies about what is a "farm animal" and what's not, what's a square or a circle, or who is a part of our family. As we grow up, we see taxonomies everywhere. Can you imagine walking into a store with your grocery list, only to find all the food spilled out all over the floor, piled up randomly? You might find the cereal you want underneath a bunch of bananas and then see a different type of cereal on the other side of the store perched on top of a stack of ground beef. It would make no sense to us (not to mention it would violate sanitation codes).

Thankfully, the grocery store employees understand the power of taxonomies. All cereals are placed together in the same aisle. You walk down it and can easily make a decision between your name-brand cereal and the off-brand cereal that might be a little cheaper. Or you can choose between the sugar cereal and the healthier option. Everything is right there for you, easily accessible and categorized.

Unfortunately, that is not the current state of HR. Our jobs are stacked up in random piles without much organization other than where someone thought they might belong. We have billions of data points about how our labor markets operate, but they cannot do us any good because they are miscategorized or hidden where we cannot find them.

This state of labor market chaos is why I started Revelio Labs, a workforce intelligence company that helps companies use workforce data to make better human capital decisions. We take all of the data out in the world—from online professional profiles to job postings to salary surveys—and put it together into one easily accessible place. You can think of us as a universal and standardized HR database.

What powers this database is our approach to categorization and taxonomies, which is the focus of this book. Where the Bloomberg Terminal revolutionized the capital markets for Wall Street, I hope that the ideas in this book will revolutionize our labor markets. My aim is for this book to help build a new foundation for a more scientific approach to allocating labor.

We have already seen results with the data we produce and the analysis we enable. Investors are using Revelio to determine which companies are a smart investment, looking at things like job retention and shifts in employment. We can use the database to compare the workforce of different cities and geographies. We can help employees get matched with jobs that are a better fit for their skill set.

We can even predict major trends that have a huge impact on our economy. For example, by looking at which pharmaceutical companies had a history of hiring for vaccine positions, we were able to accurately predict that Pfizer would be the first company to bring a COVID-19 vaccine to market.

Appropriately embedding taxonomies into our human capital management will offer all of these benefits. This book walk us through how to do this in three parts:

- Part I covers the theory of taxonomies to lay a foundation for your understanding of how taxonomies can support a revolution in human capital while also supporting your organization in better decision-making. This part includes a discussion of the fundamentals of why we even have jobs at all, why we construct jobs in the way we do, and what recent trends in technology mean for the future of work.

- Part II is more practical and covers how to build taxonomies. This part identifies the fundamental elements of implementing taxonomies within an organization and creating standardization across industries and markets.
- Part III is about how to implement taxonomies within the organization. It offers guidance and best practices for leaders, including executives and HR professionals.

This book offers a better path forward for our labor markets, aligning them with the modern approach to analysis and capital allocation that we see in capital markets. Taxonomies will transform not only human resources—offering a powerful tool to the hardworking HR professionals and other employees within People Analytics Departments—but the way we think about work.

Taxonomies will be good for employees, good for companies, and good for the entire economy. The chapters that follow introduce what taxonomies can do for you and your company. If you want to learn more, Revelio Labs has many more resources on our website: reveliolabs.com.

PART I

The Theory of Taxonomies

THIS PART OFFERS the reader a foundational understanding of a theory of work and why the human capital markets developed as they did. It analyzes historical developments and important trends to provide the reader with the core elements needed for the implementation of taxonomies within a company or across an economy. The chapters in this part allow the reader to fully grasp the more tactical recommendations presented in Part II.

1

The Architecture of Work

IN MY FIRST job after completing my PhD, I joined IBM, which had a mess of data when it came to human resources and the categorization of its employees. In the Chief Analytics Office, my colleagues and I were essentially working in a house of cards that was built bit by bit over the years by employees who were not following a standardized blueprint.

IBM is a massive company that grew by hiring employees based on immediate needs, without much thought to the future of the workforce or how to think about employees' growth—which is how most companies operate as they grow and change.

Why is this? Because leadership teams are focused on building their customer base and growing the company. They don't have time to worry about things like job categories or taxonomies. They need employees in the door to get the immediate job at hand done.

Without clear categories for the types of jobs they are hiring for, companies tend to hire a lot of team members who are not great fits. Mishiring is a common challenge for growing companies—they have a lot of immediate needs and hire accordingly to fill them. Companies wanted to attract more customers, so they built out their marketing team. They needed to ensure a quality product, so they built out a team with experience in quality control.

After these team members get in the door, however, company leaders might discover that they overhired for certain teams, like quality control, and that they actually need more marketing to bring in more customers and more revenue. They find that they actually need to invest more in customer engagement as well, because they have a lot of customer attrition and need to create more repeat customers.

When they do hire someone, though, the job needs to be categorized. If they bring on a customer solutions associate, for example, they need to know where that person would fit within the structure of the organization. When any company is in its early growth stage, that categorization is a relatively straightforward process: The new hire is situated in the appropriate place within the org chart. The customer solutions associate, for example, would likely fall under their VP of customer experience.

But as companies get bigger and grow into massive corporations like IBM, the house of cards grows and quickly becomes unwieldy. The VP of customer experience becomes the chief customer officer, with multiple VPs now reporting to that position. Those VPs oversee teams of dozens of employees. People begin to report to different leaders. But because that's the way it has always done it, the HR team continues to rely on the org chart for categorization.

Or when a company decides to create a People Analytics Department and bring on someone like me onto their team, that department becomes a whole new branch of the org chart under the Chief Human Resources Office. Someone like me comes on board and starts sorting through the house of cards the company inherited, which leads to all sorts of problems with data analysis and recommendations.

If companies can take a more standardized approach to job categorization, they can be more thoughtful and deliberate about their hiring plans. They can create job descriptions that more accurately meet the needs of the company and hire people who are better fits for those roles. They will save money in bringing on new hires and increase retention among employees. Without a standardized approach, when they hire a new person, they add that person as one more card on top of the house they have already built. The structure becomes more unwieldy and rickety with each new hire or new team added to the company.

How did we get to the point where companies are operating with such unwieldy and unscientific structures? This chapter gives you some important background on the theory of work and the science of management, including some important definitions I'll use throughout the book. It also demonstrates how labor markets refused to evolve while capital markets did.

I'll begin by talking about one man who revolutionized the way we think about work with one simple tool: a stopwatch.

An Engineer and His Stopwatch

Frederick Winslow Taylor was a mechanical engineer in the 1870s and is considered the pioneer of management consulting. He came from an impressive pedigree: He attended the exclusive Phillips Exeter Academy as a young man and had plans to attend Harvard before following in the footsteps of his father and becoming a lawyer.

That all changed, though, when instead he decided to take a job on the floor of a pump factory, which was owned by friends of his family. He continued down this path of manual labor, becoming a machinist and eventually a foreman and chief engineer.

It was through his work on the floor that he noticed his fellow laborers were not working as hard as they could. As foreman, he pushed the machinists to work harder. He obsessively studied the work they were doing and identified ways to increase their output.

His recommendations seemed unorthodox because people at the time assumed that the only way to increase productivity was through an increase of human brute-force strength. Taylor changed this thinking by making recommendations about the tools and processes being used, such as the way equipment was designed or the way that foremen should manage their workforces. Taylor's recommendations were quite specific in scope: At one point, he determined that the optimal shovel load was 21½ pounds, and he found—through repeated tests—the perfect shovel to scoop that exact amount.

What Taylor is most famous for was his stopwatch experiment. He would go to factory floors equipped with a stopwatch and time workers based on how long they took to complete tasks, sometimes down to the hundredth of a minute.

This process helped him understand the work being done and, therefore, how to maximize the productivity of workers.

Taylor died relatively young, at the age of 59 in 1915, of pneumonia, before he could see how his ideas would be taken up in industries around the world. The influence of his work continued, though. Those he worked with and influenced applied his lessons to other companies and situations. (Henry Gantt, of Gantt Chart fame, was a disciple of Taylor and applied his findings to his own research on management.)

The discipline of scientific management grew from Taylor's body of work, as employers realized that they could use scientific processes to maximize labor productivity. This concept may seem simple for us now, over 100 years later, but it was revolutionary for the time. In Taylor's time, the word "productivity" was not even in employers' vocabulary. They literally had no concept of the idea of maximizing the work of labor for an increased output.

Taylor's work was influential to many aspects of our economy, but especially in one way: breaking down and understanding the components of work. Prior to his observations, the work done by a laborer was seen as almost immutable: What someone did with their hands was all they could produce. People could work harder and faster, or slower and shirk responsibilities, but on the whole, there was not much to be done to systematically change the work completed by a single individual.

By breaking down the tasks being completed by people on a factory floor, Taylor gave us a way to think about "labor" differently. Someone was not just completing a job but was executing discrete tasks that created the sum total of that person's work.

What Taylor was observing on those factory floors, with men shoveling coal or dirt or whatever other raw materials they were using at the time, is still relevant today. What he did in breaking up discrete tasks from the overall work of laborers over a day, we can do for anyone's job today, no matter how complex. Without Taylor, we would not understand the component parts that are critical for developing taxonomies.

The Elements of Work

What Taylor had identified, by looking at the discrete tasks laborers completed, are what are called "work activities." These are defined as the pieces of work that someone does. Most of the work being done during Taylor's time was manual labor, like shoveling, assembling different components of a piece of equipment, or packing boxes. Now most of our work is considered "knowledge work," which is more focused on the relational and managerial aspects of work, such as connecting people to solve a problem, managing a project, or sending communications through emails or other digital platforms. While the work looks very different, the process of completing work activities is the same.

Work activities are the components of a job. A *job* is, essentially, a bundle of work activities. If you have a job, that means you complete a set of work activities repeatedly. You work each day and execute on specific tasks, like sending emails, managing meetings, scooping ice cream, assembling parts into cars, or whatever your job might entail. These tasks are the work activities that make up your job. With a job, you have a formal relationship with your employer, in which you are provided with a wage or salary for completing those activities. In this way, a job is also a transaction between employer and employee.

If you are shoveling coal into a furnace all day, your job could be furnace laborer, and the collection of work activities you would complete would be moving coal from one place to another, hauling coal from a delivery train or truck into the factory, and ensuring the furnace remains at a steady temperature all day. If you spend your days making sure that a company's projects are on-task, you could be a project manager and your work activities would include sending emails, drafting meeting agendas, following up with other coworkers to ensure they are on task, and so on.

In addition to completing work activities, employees also have a set of skills that help prepare them for their jobs. *Skills* are the attributes of a person that help them complete their work activities and excel at their jobs. The concept of a skill can be hard to nail down, especially because "skill" is a word we use frequently in our day-to-day conversation. Skills can arise out of some innate ability (such as physical dexterity or comfort with public speaking) but also can be honed with practice and education (such as apprenticeships or acquiring a degree). Someone can have a skill at a certain type of job or work activity, in the same way that they would have a skill for playing a musical instrument or some sport.

Figure 1.1 illustrates the connections between these components. As you can see, activities serve as the components of a job, and skills serve as attributes of people who fill those jobs.

Finally, a cluster of jobs makes up an *occupation*. You could have a job as a tax attorney, but your occupation is lawyer. Your job might be social media manager, but your occupation is communications or marketing. Clusters of

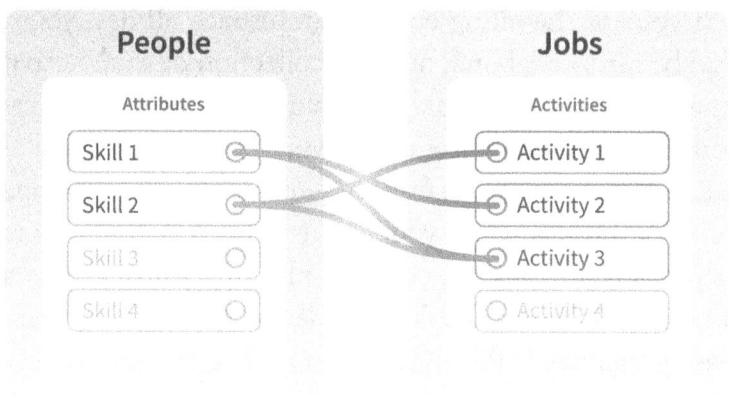

Figure 1.1 How skills, jobs, and activities are connected

jobs can be either broad or granular. Lawyer is a relatively broad cluster of jobs, but you could have a more specific cluster, such as corporate attorney. Within that you would find tax attorney, which itself could even been a cluster that contains more specific jobs, such as attorneys who specialize in limited liability corporations, multinational corporations, or public companies. In this way, taxonomies can be hierarchical in nature.

Standardization in Capital Markets

In the introduction, I shared a little bit about how capital markets became more efficient through the standardization of company data and the transparency that arose because of that standardization. The Securities and Exchange Commission was a big part of this standardization, helping force companies to align on their reporting standards to help the capital markets compare and contrast companies.

This standardization led to the rise of the accounting profession, which helped to standardize reporting across companies while providing the economy with a legion of professionals who understand the nuances of the capital markets. Even with transparency and standardization, there are many decisions that a company must make that can be incredibly complex. Assets depreciate sooner than expected, bonds transform into some other debt, and financing terms change. Accountants help keep all of this in order.

Executives have armies of accountants at their disposal to tell them anything they want to know about their capital investments—the depreciation levels of their manufacturing equipment, the state of their fleets of trucks or transportation equipment, or progress on the construction of a building. When it comes to the workforce, though, they likely can capture only qualitative information assembled from perspectives and assessments by managers. Sometimes they don't even have this data.

The current accounting function has been professionalized over the last century as our capital markets have become more efficient. Wall Street and the financial markets have become a data-driven industry. The armies of accountants can take data to ensure that what is happening at a company is standardized and clear for anyone who wants to use the data. Documents like financial statements, the balance sheet, the income statement, and the statement of cash flows can all be compared to those of any other company. Auditors ensure that these documents are correct based on company activity and appropriately aligned with necessary accounting standards. When outsiders look at these documents, they can know exactly what to make of them.

Investors use this standardized approach to determine what they believe would be a good use of capital. If these investors decide, based on the data, that a company is not doing the right thing, then they will not invest capital into the company. If they see something in the data that makes them think they will get a return on their investment, then they will provide the company with an investment.

Creating a similar, standardized approach for the labor markets is a lot more complicated. Standardization of data and appropriate categorization, alongside transparency of sharing the data, are required.

A Lack of Standardization in Labor Markets

We missed an opportunity at the birth of management science for the labor markets to keep up as the economy changed. When the accounting profession better categorized capital, allowing for smarter analysis and a more professionalized investment industry, labor markets were left behind. Taylor offered us an understanding of how to do this categorization, through his segmenting of work, but instead of building on these insights, our understanding of labor remained stuck in a turn-of-the-century mindset.

The Department of Labor attempted its first categorization of jobs when it published the *Dictionary of Occupational Titles* in the 1930s. It was exactly what it sounded like: a big book of the titles of all occupations, or as many as researchers could capture at the time. This book helped define over 13,000 jobs and was updated regularly by the government.

However, while it was regularly updated, the *Dictionary of Occupational Titles* (or *DOT*, as it was called) did not appropriately adapt to the times. It was first created to categorize and standardize many blue-collar jobs, to help with workers' comp claims and other labor-related issues. As we shifted toward a more knowledge-based economy, the definitions and standardizations became obsolete. The government created the Occupational Information Network (O*NET) as an online database, but the static nature of the *DOT* was transferred to this new digital system. The *DOT* did not reflect the rapidly changing nature of the economy, and O*NET continued this static approach to the labor markets in the 21st century.

One of the big downsides of *DOT* and later O*NET was what was originally perceived as the strength of these categorizations: They were designed to be universal. The researchers from the Department of Labor wanted to create a comprehensive list of all jobs that could be applicable to any company. For example, they defined jobs such as landscape worker, floor sander, or agriculture equipment worker and detailed what skills, knowledge, abilities, and tasks would be contained within those jobs.

But here's the problem: Not all companies care about all jobs. If you are a nail factory, you do not care about software engineers. If you run a tech start-up, you probably do not care about job categories connected to teaching or education. All that you care about are the jobs related to your company and the people you want to employ.

O*NET and other standardized labor data sources have not taken advantage of the advancement in technologies in the same way that the capital markets have, with their Bloomberg Terminals ranging across Wall Street. Instead, the labor markets are stuck with what's basically not better than a list of definitions grounded in some research from the 1930s.

Part of the reason that advances in capital production—such as the assembly line or more automation in machinery—were so successful at boosting productivity was because we understood what capital needed to go where. There was transparency in the categorization of capital, which allowed it to be moved around efficiently. When a company wanted to replace its outdated assembly line with one with more automation, it could do so relatively easily through an infusion of capital. The management team understood what it would take to upgrade the assembly line machinery and could rely on a wealth of existing information to help with that switch.

Now, as we try to implement AI and other technologies to augment our workforce, we cannot make that same seamless transition, because we do not fundamentally understand how our workforce is categorized. We cannot leverage our human capital, and shift it, in the same ways we did with physical capital.

AI and other technologies do offer an opportunity, however, to modernize our labor markets in the same way that capital markets were professionalized over the 1900s. Using AI to better segment and categorize our work can offer more robust data analyses, akin to how capital is now managed.

Now that you have a basic understanding of human capital markets and how our labor markets evolved into their current state, we can go deeper into how jobs are structured, how they transform, and what technologies can do to help manage that transformation.

2

Why Work Gets Organized into Jobs

A RECENT TREND in computer software is the development of microservices. *Microservices* are segmented programming tasks that can all run together, automatically, through an orchestration program. Microservices are all around us, operating behind much of the software we use each day. Instead of a computer program running one discrete service, now many programs are written to orchestrate multiple programs together at once. If you run a retail site, for example, you can set up an orchestration program to run microservices like order processing, payment, and inventory management together. Payment takes in the number that is being paid, stores it, and then sends that number to another database that validates it, then validates the credit card information, and then communicates with the bank.

I'll share an example of how microservices work from my own company. Our major product is a dashboard of data that companies can use to analyze their workforce and compare it to competitors. This dashboard executes on thousands of tasks for each company, automatically. When people open up the dashboard, they visit their "Company Overview" page, which offers data analysis on headcount, growth of employees, active posting for jobs, benefits, business outlook, and more.

For each of these analyses, our programmers have coded several different "microservices" that pull the Company Overview data from a massive table. These microservices execute on the command to find this data and put it together in a way that's actionable for customers. But that's not enough. The microservices also need to translate that data, through other programs, so that it can be visualized and presented in a way that's easily understood.

All of this execution occurs during the time the customer's screen loads. No one actually sees these microservices working together in concert, but there's a set of programs operating to get customers the data they need, almost in real time. Each individual programming task would be meaningless without the coordinating program orchestrating everything to ensure that customers receive a seamless and quality dashboard. Without the coordinating program, customers would be looking at a string of numbers in a table with no real meaning.

I share the example of this type of programming to offer a comparison to how jobs function. In the case of work, the *microservice* is a specific job task. The *job* is a collection of those tasks that need to be orchestrated. The *orchestrator* is not a piece of software but, instead, the employee. We can expand this example out even further, beyond just the work tasks of one employee. In this case, the orchestrator is the manager of those employees, ensuring they all complete their work tasks together in concert.

This concept of orchestration is why the nature of jobs is so important and also so complex. A common trend right now is to outsource tasks to freelancers in the hopes of streamlining work. The idea is that, instead of hiring employees to complete a set of tasks, a company can outsource the work to a series of contractors to save money on employees. Rather than hiring a graphic designer as a full-time employee, for example, a company can hire one person to create a logo, one person to create graphics for a website, and one person to create printed marketing materials. Contracting out these tasks could be an appealing option for a company, because it does not need to go through the process of hiring and onboarding someone. You assign the task, and it's done.

Yet trying to contract out through gig workers creates a complete mess. I'll extend the example out even further, beyond the area of graphic design, to show why. You could hire freelancers to collect different datasets, manage calendars, schedule meetings, and plan events. You name it—you can hire someone to do it. A company that operates in this way has created a company that has a 100% work-on-demand approach.

Without someone overseeing all the work, there will be so many inefficiencies within the company that it's highly unlikely anything will get done. First, the negotiation of prices for each of the tasks will be all-consuming. Instead of negotiating a salary for one employee, the head of the company will have to negotiate each task completed (unless, of course, the head of the company decides to contract out that negotiation as well). Then there will be the time-intensive information exchange required for each task. The contractor working on the logo will have to coordinate with the person laying out the marketing materials. Maybe there is a change in the logo colors, which requires a change in the marketing materials, but that is not communicated in enough time, and when the contractor working on the marking materials finally gets this information, the person has to go back and start all over.

All of this also says nothing about who will review everything and ensure it meets the appropriate standards. Is the head of the company doing these reviews? Or will this all be contracted out as well?

Pretty soon, work has ground to a halt because no one has enough information or guidance to get anything done.

The value of orchestration is fundamentally why we need jobs in our economy. Without them, things fall apart. This chapter builds on the foundational elements of theory introduced in Chapter 1 to discuss the theory of why we need jobs, why we aren't just individual task rabbits working on uncoordinated activities all day, and how taxonomies can help to make the orchestration of tasks contained within a job or a team run more smoothly. The chapter also includes a discussion of "bundling," which is important not only to the development of taxonomies but also to the management of the workforce.

The Value of Firms: Ronald Coase and the Nature of the Firm

If we want to know why we need jobs, then we need to ask a bigger question: Why do we even need companies? To find the answer, we can look to the first person to tackle this important question: Ronald Coase.

Coase was a British economist, born around the same time that Frederick Winslow Taylor's ideas about productivity and scientific management were taking off. He and his peers were tackling some of the biggest questions about how our world worked. Coase took on an important question within the burgeoning field of economics: When does it make sense to use markets, and when is more of a command-and-control approach appropriate?

Coase explored this question through the model of a firm. The idea that anyone would start a company or a firm can be quite puzzling. The entrepreneur who does this takes on unnecessary overhead costs: buildings, heat, supplies, and, most expensive, employees and managers. Why would anyone hire a person merely to manage other people rather than to get necessary work done? Surely it would be cheaper just to contract out that work to individuals who are very good at executing on those tasks, reducing overhead costs.

In his seminal piece, "The Nature of the Firm," written in 1937, Coase showed that it was, in fact, rational to create a firm, due to the massive levels of transaction costs that would come with contracting out work in a marketplace, as I illustrated earlier. If we were to have a massive marketplace where everyone could sell their services as individual contractors, massive inefficiencies would be created due to all the time (and money) spent to try to orchestrate all those individual contractors together.

The Challenges of Unbundling Work

What Coase described in his article was the difference between "bundled" and "unbundled" work. *Bundled work* is work done by a single individual—the work is all "bundled" together in a job. A company would hire someone as a graphic designer to complete any image-related marketing tasks rather than contracting out the logo, the printed materials, the website, and so on. The Graphic Designer, essentially, becomes the "coordinator" of the work, playing the role of the orchestration program in the microservices example at the beginning of the chapter.

A marketplace where every task is contracted out does not have the work coordinated or orchestrated; it is an "unbundled" market.

Let's look at a very simple example to show what an unbundled marketplace might look like.

Imagine you are an entrepreneur who wants to sell one specific product to customers: lemonade. To sell this product successfully, you need to purchase your inputs (lemons, water, sugar) and turn these into your output (lemonade). You need to acquire materials to transfer the inputs into outputs, which means you need some kind of bowls, lemon squeezers, measuring cups, and something to stir. You need something to store the lemonade in to sell it to customers. You also need some way to let customers know about your product (marketing). And you need some way to process payments from customers. (You also probably will need someone to find you a storefront and manage the space, not to mention a way to store your revenue, project cash flow, plan for future growth, etc., but let's focus our example just on the customer transaction.)

Phew! That's a lot of work. Lucky for you, there is a robust marketplace of individual contractors who can perform each one of those tasks. You contract out and get one person for each task and open your doors for business.

Well, the first day is a complete mess. The person who buys your inputs purchases too many lemons, not enough water, and way too much sugar. The person making the lemonade quickly runs out of water, and the leftover sugar starts attracting bugs in your store. The equipment purchased isn't useful for the person making the lemonade, because the squeezer makes his hand cramp up. The person you contracted to do marketing was way too ambitious, and you have too many customers to handle. These customers all wait outside in the hot sun and give up after half an hour. They tell all their friends not to come to your store.

Your lemonade business is done before it even gets started.

This is a simple (and silly) example, but it represents an extreme example of what Coase was talking about. There is value in firms orchestrating tasks, because without that orchestration, inefficiencies are created and things can get complicated quickly.

In the same way that a firm cannot contract out all its work, a company cannot unbundle tasks from a job. Doing so will spread everything out into an internal market in a company or organization, leading to similar problems and inefficiencies as your lemonade stand.

The big idea from Coase's article is that a market of contractors has costly coordination costs, but those do not exist in an environment like a firm. When a job is not orchestrated, more time is spent coordinating among five people doing five things rather than one person doing five things. If the person who bought the materials for the lemonade was the same person who was making the lemonade, she would have known exactly what she needed and what equipment was best suited for her, and things probably would have gone a lot more smoothly at your store.

The Case for Managers

Many times people on the receiving end of this orchestration feel like this type of coordination is redundant and unnecessary. How many times do employees complain about the number of meetings they must attend or about a middle manager looking over their shoulders as they work?

Certainly, meetings can be streamlined and micromanagement is counterproductive. However, some level of coordination and alignment is required to allow companies to operate efficiently. In his book *Work Rules!*, Laszlo Bock, the former senior vice president of people operations at Google, discusses how his former employer ran some experiments on how to best manage work within the company. Some teams operated within a more deconstructed framework, where employees contracted out more work using an "unbundled" marketplace of tasks. Other teams operated within a more traditional model with managers orchestrating work tasks through oversight.[1]

Guess which one performed better? The teams with managers.

Work needs a conductor. Bock's experience at Google tracks with Coase's theoretical findings and shows that we cannot "unbundle" jobs and hope that a market will take care of the work for us. This is why we continue to rely on middle management, no matter how much people complain about it.

The notion of bundling has implications that I will return to throughout the book, such as how much AI can automate work. Certainly some tasks can be unbundled and automated through software, but whenever something becomes unbundled, there will always need to be someone to help orchestrate that work to ensure it's completed in the appropriate ways.

Categorization and the Art of Bundling Work

It's easy to see why companies end up without clarity on the most effective ways to bundle work. When you step back and consider the complexity of bundling jobs, you can see why most companies struggle with categorization and bundling. Most companies require thousands of tasks—and, in some cases, hundreds of millions of tasks—to complete their business every day. One worker by him- or herself probably completes over a dozen distinct activities in a day, and a large corporation can employ hundreds of thousands of people.

Let's consider what it would take for one person actually to complete everything required in a company. Such a person would have to be some kind of superworker, with no constraints on time and no limit to their mental or physical energy. The person could complete all the tasks, and take all the time needed, until the work got done.

Obviously, no superworker exists who can complete all the tasks required in a large company. But, in smaller companies, we can get closer to that idea of a superworker because there is just less to get done. About 10% of all businesses in the United States—over 800,000 companies—are sole proprietorships,[2] meaning that only one person works there, which in almost all cases is the owner of the company. In these companies, that one worker probably can do all the tasks required, because that's how the company has been arranged. These are probably freelance companies—like a virtual assistant who helps manage scheduling for multiple clients. But this single employee also takes care of marketing, client management, bookkeeping, and all of the other necessary tasks to keep a company in business.

For larger companies, though, we need to divide up the tasks and categorize them appropriately to make the orchestration of work between jobs flow seamlessly. Why is categorization important when bundling tasks for jobs? Consider the alternative: Let's say we just randomly assign tasks into bundles and create jobs from there. We'd end up with one single person completing tasks like legal filings alongside recruiting alongside equipment repair (depending on the size and scope of the company). Good luck finding one person with the skills to do all that!

But let's say there is someone who happens to have the required skills to do legal filings, recruitment, and equipment repair. Even if a person has those seemingly disparate skills, there can also be a natural complementarity between the execution of tasks that makes it more efficient to group similar tasks together as a job. If we extend our hypothetical, think about the person who has to run from a recruitment meeting to the factory floor to repair some equipment and then head down to the courtroom to deal with some legal issues. That takes up a lot of unnecessary time. If these tasks were instead grouped together, so that equipment repair goes with equipment operation, recruitment goes with benefits management, and legal filings goes with contract negotiation, those jobs can be orchestrated more easily and efficiently.

Taking a standardized approach to bundling work requires thoughtful consideration about which categories for jobs make sense. Most companies haven't taken this step yet.

Amazon and the "Two Pizza" Rule

Let's consider a real example of a company that was able to successfully categorize and bundle its work in a specific way to reap the benefits.

Jeff Bezos, Amazon founder and CEO, has talked about how he likes to keep his teams as small as possible: No more than you can feed with two pizzas.[3] The smaller teams at Amazon have created individualized "silos" of work across the company that operate independently of each other.

Creating smaller teams, and siloing off the work, seems counterintuitive to the idea of bundling and categorization. If we want to group work together to reduce the transaction costs between employees and teams, shouldn't we also want to group employees together into a hierarchy that streamlines orchestration?

Many companies have taken this approach, particularly larger, multinational corporations like my old employer, IBM. They have a command-and-control structure, which has clear lines of authority and reporting up the chain of command into the C-suite. When I was at IBM, we spent a lot of time trying to exchange information and understand what other teams were doing. If another team reported to the same VP as yours, you needed to know what was happening with them to make sure your work was all aligned.

Amazon has a much flatter structure, as compared to these command-and-control companies, which might indicate teams at Amazon spend a lot more time spent understanding what other teams are doing. More teams lead to a greater need for coordination, right?

In fact, the exact opposite is true. By breaking up their work into smaller teams, Amazon has identified the right ways to bundle their work, balancing the need for coordination and orchestration. There can be some redundancies with coordination, but that is the trade-off for the ability to scale faster. Their teams are just the right size, with the right bundling of tasks and employees, so that the different silos can operate more or less operate independently of each other with little need for coordination across teams.[4]

Amazon has more than a million employees (globally) but it can still operate efficiently, without massive transaction costs, to ensure that everyone is aligned in their work because of the size of their teams and their understanding of how to best bundle work. The Amazon Web Services (AWS) business line is the best example of the output of rightsizing for coordination and orchestration. Amazon identified a need to scale up its computing power, and it had a set of teams tackle this problem through the development of various cloud computing offerings. It found that other companies also had this need for cloud computing software, so Amazon began offering it as a service externally. AWS is now one of Amazon's most profitable divisions.

Amazon probably would not have been able to create this business line if it had the traditional hierarchical approach to work. With a modular talent system, the company can take on new work without overcomplicating operations or slowing down their execution.

How to Bundle Work

Now that we understand the need to bundle work, let's consider what types of work should be bundled together.

Bundling Tasks Within the Same Process

If work tasks are part of the same process, that's a good indication that the work should be bundled together into a job or set of jobs on the same teams. If there's a chain of work tasks that needs to be completed—A needs to be done, then

B, and then when B is done, you can do C, and so on—then it makes sense for one person to complete those tasks or for a group of people to do those tasks together if the tasks are too complicated for one person to handle.

Here's a simple example: social media management. While it may seem straightforward, there are many steps to complete the group of activities that make up managing a company's social media feed. First, the social media post needs to be written. Then it needs to be posted on the social media site. Then it needs to be monitored for any responses or reactions from followers.

Theoretically, a separate person could do each of these tasks on their own. An employee may want to write the posts but has no interest in dealing with the technical challenges of managing the platform itself. Perhaps this is an older employee who is comfortable writing but isn't tech savvy enough to figure out how to use the social media platforms. Or maybe the social posts are more graphic-heavy, so a graphic designer creates the posts, but that person isn't good at responding to the comments after the post goes live.

But, in practice, dividing these tasks up can be very complicated. If three people were completing these three tasks, they would spend a lot of time talking to each other about how to do their jobs. There would be a high transaction cost with this sharing of information. The person managing the responses in the comments might not understand the original post itself, and to complete his tasks, he would essentially require the person who created the original post to explain exactly what she did and why, which would essentially duplicate her work. If you imagine a company has not one social media feed but several across platforms, with hundreds of comments and engagements a day, you can see how this coordination would get out of hand quickly.

Tasks within social media management mostly exist within the same process, which is why they are usually grouped together into one job, a social media manager, who handles the full life cycle of these tasks, reducing coordination costs and information exchange.

Bundling Tasks That Require Common Skills and Interests

Another reason to bundle tasks together is based on the common skills and interests required to complete them. This categorization is intuitive and how most companies design their jobs. If someone has a skill in writing social media posts, for example, they probably have skills in other communication areas, like blog posts. A grouping of similar skills is how you get jobs like communications associate or marketing associate, which combine tasks like managing a blog, social media feed, and newsletter. Grouping work in this way also has the added benefit of aligning with an employee's interest—in this case, a communications associate probably enjoys writing, for example.

Grouping work activities based on common skills and interests may have nothing to do with the work products and may have more to do with the technical expertise required to complete the work processes. The job of lawyer is a great example of this way of bundling. If you are a trained lawyer, you probably can complete the task of reviewing sales contracts as well as something completely unrelated, such as the task of developing a privacy agreement. These tasks have basically nothing to do with each other, but they require the same skill set and expertise of understanding the law.

How these jobs are bundled and to what degree of specificity will depend on the size and need of a company. A small firm may hire one lawyer to look at all of its legal documents. A larger multinational company may have hundreds of lawyers on staff, segmented further based on specific needs. The large company could have a contracts department, or a privacy department, within their legal division, for example.

The challenge with skill-based jobs is that skills and interests don't always align. As a lawyer, you may be able to do contract law, but maybe you hate it, and instead you want to make policy recommendations. If you are put into a position where you are reviewing contracts every day, you may end up quitting or doing a bad job. Or you may love being the only lawyer at that small firm because you get to do a little bit of everything. (The changing desires of employees connects to the idea of job transformation, the subject of the next chapter.)

Bundling Tasks That Can Reduce the Cost of Hiring

Hiring is expensive. Sometimes it makes more sense for one person to do a broader bundle of tasks that are loosely connected than to hire another person who may be better equipped to handle the tasks. In the case of lawyers, for example, if a company needs a lawyer to review sales contracts as well as privacy agreements, they could hire two people and have them specialize. Or they could hire one person, even if that new hire is not particularly skilled at one part of the job. It's cheaper to do it that way.

The cost of hiring is also why you sometimes have people working more than double the hours of what is typically expected for someone in a full-time job. The lawyer example is a good one to illustrate this point. Many corporate lawyers work well beyond 80 hours a week, sometimes putting in 100 hours a week. Certainly these individuals are not as efficient at their 100th hour as they are at their 41st hour. There are tremendous diminishing returns when someone is working a 100-hour workweek. However, it would still make sense to bundle these many work tasks into one job if the cost of hiring (and retaining) an additional employee would be that much higher than the value lost from having someone work those long hours.

Bundling Tasks That Can Reduce the Cost of Sharing Information

Sometimes the tasks required to complete a job are so specific, and require so much specialized knowledge to understand, that it makes sense for one person to complete all of the tasks, no matter how much time it takes or how many other orchestration costs go along with it. In these roles, the cost of sharing information about different work tasks between people is so high it makes sense to keep everything contained in one job.

These are typically jobs—like lawyers—where a high premium is placed on access to the individual completing the tasks. Claudia Goldin called this "greedy work"; a professional is required to spend long hours in a job, practically always on call, in exchange for an exorbitant amount of money.[5] These people are overseeing large deals, like a merger and acquisition process for a business, or working on a high-profile legal case. Something could happen at any hour of the day, and this person is expected to be there to complete whatever task may be asked of them.

I have personally benefited from this type of bundled job: My company was undertaking a Series A fundraising round, and we hit a snag with some of the legal documentation just as we were about to finalize everything. We had to call one of our lawyers to help finalize the deal, even though he was on vacation in Europe with his family. He took the call from his hotel bathroom while his family slept in the bedroom. We were very happy to pay him whatever he thought it was worth to complete that task, because without his work, we would not have closed our funding round. Literally no one else in the world would have been able to do the work he did.

There are less extreme examples of the value of information sharing leading to a bundling of jobs. Again, I will use another personal example: My company no longer hires part-time employees. I operate a relatively technical and complicated company, which requires a lot of background information to complete tasks successfully. Often the first 15 hours in a week are spent just understanding the latest developments of other teams as well as developments in the market. If we were to have someone work for only 20 hours a week, we'd get only 5 hours of productivity. (This is a simplified example, of course.) So it makes much more sense for us to bundle more tasks into a full-time job to ensure that we maximize the productivity of our employees.

Bundling Tasks That Can Create a Shared Language

It's not enough merely to bundle work and leave it at that, however. You also need to call it something. Theoretically, a company could create one bundle of work activities and call it "Job A" and the next one "Job B," and so on.

But that would create all other kinds of problems. For one, job seekers would see a job posting for "Job A" and not know if they would be interested in that job or not. If, instead, the job was labeled lawyer or, even better, criminal defense attorney, then there would be a much better chance of your company finding a qualified candidate to complete the tasks associated with the bundle of work activities with that specific label.

Appropriate labeling helps the labor market to function. A product manager at one company can be different enough from a product manager at another company that the employees are functionally doing different jobs. Markets work only when good information can flow from buyers (companies) and sellers (employees). That information can flow only when all parties are speaking the same language—in this case, with standardized job titles.

Standardized labels and titles have another benefit that I speak more to later in the book: namely, that similar labels and categories can help us to understand the nature of the work being completed.

Now that we understand why it makes sense to bundle work and how to think about which work tasks should be bundled, we can begin to explore one critical component of the theory of work: job transformation.

3

How Jobs Transform

Is a tomato a fruit or a vegetable?

This question is surprisingly controversial. Depending on how you think about it, the answer can be either. A tomato can be a fruit or a vegetable. It depends.

Some of you reading this may now be screaming at your book. How can I even be asking this question? Of course a tomato is a fruit! It's science! Fruits have seeds, tomatoes have seeds, so tomatoes are fruit. End of story.

That is true. But here's how I classify the differences between fruits and vegetables: If it goes into a salad, it's a vegetable. Using this form of classification, then a tomato is definitely a vegetable.

Well, you may ask, what about blue cheese? Or croutons? Or the apple slices and cranberries I sometimes put in my green salad? Are those vegetables?

And to that I would say: Those don't count. They are very obviously not vegetables.

If you haven't yet thrown your book across the room in frustration, maybe this was the last straw. How can I, a person who wrote a whole book about taxonomies, dismiss classification categories this easily?

But here's the thing about classifications and taxonomies: We categorize things to help us make sense of them. If the categorization helps us achieve that goal, then it's useful. If it doesn't, then it's not.

This tomato example is important to keep in mind as we continue to explore how to classify jobs. Because jobs—and the work activities that are bundled to create those jobs—are not static things. They change and evolve. For that reason, the categories must change as well.

Think about the changing nature of how we think about "dogs." At one time, dogs would have been closer in category to wolves. Prehistoric humans would have wanted nothing to do with them. We would have seen them as an active threat to our survival and put them in the category of "predator." The wild dogs that remain in parts of sub-Saharan Africa are still categorized as predators because they actively hunt other animals, as any predator does.

But, at some point, how we think of "dog" changed. Now we consider them as pets. They are no longer a threat to us, and many of us welcome them into our homes. We make them a part of our families, even sometimes placing them at the same level in our family hierarchies as our children.

As we grow from children to adults and understand the world differently, categories can also shift. I have two young kids, and one of the first taxonomies we introduced to them was the category of "farm animal." They understood that animals like cows, chickens, and horses all fit into this category. However, as my children age, I doubt they will spend much time on a farm, interacting with these animals that have very little connection to each other. How they categorize these animals will probably change as well. They may categorize horses with antelope and deer, as those animals obviously have more in common with a horse than a pig does.

In the same way, job categories change over time. Job categories transform because the nature of work transforms. This transformation can come from external market forces, requiring a different type of work (in the age of AI, how many transcriptionists are gainfully employed?), or from employee desires (an executive assistant who wants to become an analyst). Jobs are always changing, because people are always changing.

To understand how taxonomies can be used to better manage the way we work, it is necessary to recognize that job transformation occurs continuously. We like to think that categorizing things makes them static and standard, but that is not true. In fact, the opposite is true. Categories are useful only when they serve a purpose, and when they no longer do, they must be changed and reconsidered.

The Accelerating Transformation of Work

Job transformation has been a feature of the workplace since the beginning of time, but lately the rate of that transformation has accelerated. Around 60% of the work being done today did not exist in the 1940s.[1]

Much of what is driving the transformation of jobs is the rapid pace of technological change. Our adoption of newer and better technologies has coincided with the shift toward more knowledge work in the past 60 years and away from the reliance on manual labor.

Central to the transformation of jobs is the complexity of knowledge work and the number of tasks contained within a job. As a coal miner, for example, you may complete three basic tasks throughout your day. But as a marketing manager, you may complete 20 tasks. The coal miner's tasks do not shift over time (shovel coal, haul coal, dump coal), but a marketing manager's tasks are based more on human interaction and human relationships. These relationships and interactions can change from day to day, leading to a complex balancing of changing tasks and the transformation of a job over time.

These transformations almost always have unexpected consequences.

Take the case of bank tellers. When automated teller machines (ATMs) were first introduced, everyone assumed it would be the end of bank tellers. The main work activity that bank tellers completed was helping customers deposit funds and withdraw money. ATMs now automated those tasks. Therefore, no more bank tellers.

But guess what happened? In the 30 years from when ATMs were introduced as a new innovation to when they became ubiquitous, the number of bank tellers employed actually went up.[2] How could that be? That finding seems completely irrational, and unexpected.

Banks were certainly not hiring more bank tellers to help their customers withdraw funds. The ATMs were doing that. Banks were instead hiring bank tellers to do something completely different. The job had changed. It had been transformed.

Comparing the classification of "Bank Teller" in the 1970s to the same position today is completely meaningless. They are no longer the same job. After ATMs came on the market, the job of bank teller became much more service-oriented. Today bank tellers help customers navigate the different products offered by the bank, understand what products might be right for them, answer questions, and open new credit cards. Bank tellers are now less focused on the numbers of customer banking—money going in and money going out—and are more relational.

Types of Transformation

Even though jobs are frequently being transformed—sometimes, like that of the bank teller, to the point of being unrecognizable—it's unlikely that someone will wake up one day and have a completely new job without warning. That can happen, but, more likely, a job transforms over time. These transformations happen in small ways building on each other until, over time, the employee or the manager or both realize that they have a completely new job.

How do these small transformations occur, leading to job transformation? There are two ways: top down and bottom up.

Top-Down Transformation

Jobs can transform because the needs of the company or organization change. This model of transformation is called "top-down" transformation, where the manager serves as a liaison between the employee and the company's business needs and assigns work based on the needs of the company (and its leadership). If a company has a new request, the manager determines who on their team is the best equipped to respond to that request. The employee then executes on that request. As the needs of the company change, the nature of the employee's work changes.

These transformations happen all the time with companies, big and small. Twitter (now X) was originally conceived of as a text messaging system within a closed group, not a social network. Then management decided to pivot to what we now know as social media. Netflix originally sent DVDs in the mail, before leadership decided to change course and build the company's massive streaming and entertainment service. During the pandemic, many companies pivoted to make masks or hand sanitizer. One owner of a vintage clothing shop in Omaha, which wasn't selling much in the way of vintage clothing anymore, decided to set up a shop on Etsy just for cloth masks.[3]

My company also evolved at the start of the pandemic. Originally we did most of our selling by attending conferences. By the end of March 2020, those conferences were all canceled. To fill this gap, I, along with other leaders, started an industry newsletter that quickly became very popular. Now that we can go to conferences again, we still invest resources into this newsletter, and it continues to pay dividends to our sales pipeline. As we evolved, the work of our employees evolved, requiring us to hire people who could execute on a newsletter strategy rather than on a conference sales strategy.

Companies can also dictate the transformation of not only *what* employees are doing but also *how* they are doing their work. Managers can transform the work of employees through the management structure of the organization and teams. Often this top-down direction happens based on updates to the body of research aimed at understanding management or on a different understanding of productivity. A CEO or manager could learn about the "agile" method of work at a conference or training and then come in the next week and have everyone in the company start using this framework. Suddenly, everyone is at a stand-up meeting first thing every day and there are sticky notes all over the office.

This kind of top-down job transformation gets a bad rap. Under the top-down model, managers can move from being a liaison between the business and employee to being a micromanager who has a heavy hand in telling how employees should do their work. Frederick Taylor—the management scientist with the stopwatch from Chapter 1—is usually cited as the first micromanager, because he would go around and determine the appropriate angle for someone to hold their shovel or chide people for not completing their tasks in the most efficient ways possible (as determined by him, of course).

To be clear, top-down management is not the same thing as micromanagement. Often a top-down approach to management is still very much grounded in the needs of the employee. The manager assesses how team members are doing with their bundle of tasks and tries to determine how they can be helped to do their work better. In this way, the manager serves less as a liaison to the business and more as a facilitator of team dynamics. If one employee is struggling with a task, another employee can pick up the slack or help train the struggling employee on how to do better.

Top-down management still gives space to follow General George Patton's advice: "Never tell people how to do things. Tell them what to do and they will surprise you with their ingenuity."[4] The top-down manager serves as a connection between employees and the rest of the organization to help employees succeed in completing their work.

As the organization changes and evolves, the manager helps employees evolve with it.

Bottom-Up Transformation (Job Crafting)

In contrast to manager-driven, top-down transformation, bottom-up transformation is driven by employees. Bottom-up transformation can be thought of as job crafting, where employees drive what they would like their jobs to be. Employees choose to do things differently in their jobs to be more satisfied in their work and to do their work more effectively.

Sometimes a desire for satisfaction leads employees to decide to complete different tasks. For example, a product manager at a software company usually serves as a liaison between the engineers and the client or customer. The product manager usually completes much more relational tasks, translating between client needs and technical limitations, than the engineer, who focuses more on coding the software product. If product managers are interested in doing more direct coding, they may shift responsibilities toward an engineering job. Or the engineer could want more interaction with clients and move into a product manager role. As the job of product managers transforms, their careers also transform at the intersection of where two different bundles of work intersect—coding responsibilities and client management responsibilities. They can move their careers forward while their work changes—in fact, much of an employee's career development comes through job transformation.

Other times, employees decide to transform their jobs because they identify opportunities for improvement in their processes. They want to do their work better, make their bosses look good, and help their employer succeed.

When I'm asked by younger professionals for career advice, I give them advice based on this bottom-up job transformation model of work and suggest they look for ways to make their workflows more efficient. By doing this, they can streamline their work and transform their jobs (and potentially transform them into more senior and higher-paying roles).

For example, if the team is handling a lot of requests that need to be turned around within 48 hours, maybe the employee can create a form that takes in information about the requests and automatically sends the requested deliverable or alerts the team if a more bespoke response is needed. Or, if there are a lot of requests for the same task over and over (e.g., Where can I find the files for the company logo?), putting all the frequently requested information into one central spot for easy access can free up time for other, more productive things.

Ambitious employees can always find new ways to be productive, which changes the nature of their work and the company's work as well. These ambitious employees are not being directed by their managers but are still serving the company and helping the organization to become more productive and efficient.

Managing Transformation

Bottom-up and top-down transformation are two ends of a spectrum. Almost always, when a job transforms, it does so through some combination of manager-led and employee-led changes—never solely one or the other. In this way, transformation occurs in a hybrid way, as a discussion between managers and employees. There is a constant collaboration going on between the manager and employee about what is truly valuable in the work, how the work is playing out in real time, and how the manager can best support the employee in executing on their tasks while also feeling fulfilled in their work. This dialogue between manager and employee about the nature of the employee's work is at the heart of the practice of management.

I'll share an example from my own career to illustrate the dual nature of this transformation. Soon after being hired at IBM as a data scientist, I was promoted. I had proved myself successful at completing the necessary tasks that came with data collection and analysis, and the company wanted me to take on more responsibility. That meant it added a new bucket of tasks to my job description: managing people.

Unfortunately, I was terrible at this newly acquired bundle of tasks. I was never taught how to manage people in my PhD program and had almost no experience doing it. Therefore, I could not successfully execute on what the company needed me to do when it came to managing other data scientists.

Because I was bad at it, I hated doing it. I desperately wanted a change. I couldn't do what the company was asking of me. I essentially needed to negotiate a job transformation.

I ended up with a higher-profile role within the company, leading our data science working group. Because I took on these responsibilities, I was able to transition out of some of my management roles. I got to do what I was good at while also meeting the needs of the company. Slowly, I got better at management through practice and support from my own manager and other resources from the company.

My journey to management is likely familiar to many people who have stepped into managerial roles. Management-bound employees are very good at a specific skill set—data science, sales, programming—and then they are promoted into a management role that has nothing to do with that skill set at all. They quickly realize they are in over their head and, if they are self-aware enough, ask for help to improve.

The opposite can happen as well. Good managers are brought back down to complete tasks they have been promoted out of. We have an excellent director of engineering at my company who manages a team of several engineers. Recently, though, we had a massive project in which we were switching database platforms to a new and better version. Our existing system was costing us a massive portion of our annual revenue, so we decided to switch to something more cost-effective.

Unfortunately, though, this database switch took a lot of work. Because our programming is so complex, specialized knowledge was required to complete the transfer to the new system, and we couldn't hire new people to take on the tasks, because the cost to train someone in our system would have been too burdensome. We also didn't have enough people to complete the tasks in house. We were burning through money and time, unable to ramp up to the new system in the way we needed.

Our director of engineering decided to step out of his management responsibilities to put his head down and just code. He elected to do this, even though he much prefers management instead of the technical aspects of coding, because the company needed him to do so. It may have cost us more for him to be in this role, in the short term, as I and others had to take on more management responsibilities. This was worth it, though, to get the project done and allow us to capture significant cost savings with the new platform. Once it was over, the director of engineering ended up back where he's most useful: as a team leader.

It's important to recognize how jobs transform because understanding that process can help us manage work toward organizational goals. Transformation is always occurring, and we need to be aware of that transformation to make sure we continue to have well-defined jobs that are helping employees operate at their maximum capacity.

Managing transformation *is* management. All managers should be, fundamentally, helping their employees to manage their job transformations, because of either their own bottom-up desires or their company's top-down demands. Managers need to always think about who on their teams is completing what tasks, who is good at what, who is interested in stretching or changing their work, and what the company needs from the team at this moment. By doing this, managers can help the team to unblock work, maximize its own productivity, and maximize the amount of work being completed.

A manager who can successfully navigate job transformation is a successful manager.

The next chapter explains in more detail a tool that managers and companies can use to help guide job transformation: technological automation and, specifically, artificial intelligence.

4

Technologies and Transformation

My mom started her career in a job you don't see at all anymore: typist.

She went to secretarial school, got certified on a specific IBM typewriter, and got a high enough words-per-minute score (85) that she was able to get a job at a law firm in Westchester County, New York. After working for several years in this role, things started to change.

Like many typists of her age, she saw the transformation of her industry. Typewriters were replaced by computers, which were easier to use and had greater functionality. Typing became expected as a basic skill set for more and more people, which meant that fewer intermediaries (typists) were required to complete basic tasks.

As the typist job went away and became automated through the personal computer and other transcription services, my mom's career didn't suffer; in fact, it took off. Because some of her tasks had become automated, she was able to take on different and more responsibilities. Her job transformed into what today we would call an administrative professional, scheduling meetings and supporting her bosses in many different ways beyond typing. Her responsibilities continued to evolve, and eventually, after moving through several different administrative roles, she ended up organizing and managing the many subsidiaries of the large holding company where she worked. She was basically in charge of a massive database, full of information about the hundreds of companies owned by her employer. She ended her career essentially as a database administrator, despite never applying for a job with the title database administrator.

The role of database administrator required more human creativity than her first job as a typist, but it was still grounded in that first role. She was originally trained on how to translate information onto a page, through words. This work shifted into translating information onto a computer screen. Then it shifted again, away from relying only on words toward organizing more complex information represented by data on companies and subsidiaries.

Throughout my mom's career, her job was transformed, sometimes based on her own motivation through bottom-up means, but it also was significantly shaped by something completely out of her control: technological advancement.

Technology is constantly shifting and changing work for many reasons. These changes are part of a major top-down transformation that affects the entire economy, not just one company or organization. (See Chapter 3.) My mom was trained on one technology—the typewriter—that was soon rendered irrelevant by the introduction of the personal computer, but itself was a disruption in the market from the previous transcription technology of pen and paper (which was also a technological disruption away from parchment and quills).

Many times, when we hear of some new technology coming onto the market, we hear about jobs being replaced by that technology. This concern goes back to the Industrial Revolution, when the steam engine threatened to replace human labor at a massive scale. The American fable of John Henry is a classic story of human labor versus machines. In the story, John Henry was a "steel driving man," who would hammer steel drill bits into rock, creating holes that would be used for explosives to clear the way for a railroad. He was pitted against a steam-powered drill machine to see who could make the most holes—man or the machine.

In the story, John Henry wins the battle against the machine but collapses from exhaustion and dies. He was able to beat the machine only at the cost of his life. His labor becomes fully replaced by new technology, even though he was more "productive" than the machine when it mattered.

Luckily, most technological disruptions don't work this way. Even tremendously powerful new technologies, like electricity, the internet, or even artificial intelligence, do not end up replacing jobs through automation. Instead, they end up *transforming* jobs through the automation of tasks that make labor more efficient.

This chapter illustrates how and in what ways technology—and disruptions to the market in general—creates job transformation. Artificial intelligence (AI) is used as a case study to show how even this most advanced of technologies will (likely) not fully automate all of our jobs away.

The Disruption of Work

Each generation has some new major technological advancement introduced during their lifetime that changes everything. For my generation, that was the internet. For my kids, that probably will be AI. I have two young daughters, and about as soon as my oldest could speak in sentences, she started asking our Alexa to do things. It would always ignore her, because it couldn't understand her. But then, one day, she asked it to play "Let It Go," from the Disney film *Frozen*, and it complied. Something had changed in her voice and articulation that allowed the technology to understand her.

As I watched her dance around to the song for probably the two hundredth time, I realized that she had just completed a task that she would probably be doing for her whole life. She was interfacing with technology as an AI native, in the same way I interfaced with the internet, or my parents interfaced with the telephone, or my grandparents interfaced with typewriters.

Each of these technologies dramatically shifted the way we work—and the way we live—so fundamentally that we cannot conceive of life without them. Can you imagine living without the internet? Or a way to call someone across the country? Or even living without electricity?

New technologies are inherently disruptive to the way we work, because they offer new and different, and usually better, ways to do our work. But many other things serve as disruptions to our way of life that can transform work, for good and bad.

One of the biggest drivers of disruption in history has been war. World War II, for example, completely shifted our conception of who can do what work, as more women entered the workforce to pick up the jobs left behind by men heading off to war. Wars have also driven the development of new technologies, which have been applied to civilian life in unexpected ways. (The internet was first developed as a project at the U.S. Department of Defense.) Wars upend social order, redraw boundaries, and, of course, incur massive loss of life.

But there are other nontechnological disruptions that are less disruptive than the nature of war. Demographic changes in society can affect how work gets done and what work gets done. As a workforce ages and is replaced by a younger generation, new workers bring new skills (comfort with new technologies) but also preferences (desire for work-life balance, an example from the current rising Gen Z). These demographic shifts change the nature of work and productivity.

Regulatory changes also transform work. For example, after the Enron scandal of the early 2000s, the government set much stricter accounting standards for businesses, which changed the way accountants do their work. Labor laws have also changed over the years to protect workers' safety, prohibiting certain dangerous types of work (such as child labor).

Similar to regulatory changes, business process changes also support disruption, although usually on a much smaller scale. Over the years, new and different ways to think about the nature of work have changed how we do our work. Taylor had his stopwatch and most efficient shovels, but management scientists are always trying to figure out better ways to get work done. The concept of Just-in-Time inventory, pioneered by Toyota, completely revolutionized manufacturing and the way we assemble goods. The minimum viable product concept—an approach popularized by Silicon Valley, in which companies rely less on business plans and more on fast-moving product launches—shifted the entire start-up landscape.

Finally, true shocks to the system, such as the COVID-19 pandemic, can shift the way we work. The pandemic disrupted all aspects of our lives and forced innovation in many ways of working. For example, working from home, at least a few days a week, was already on the rise, but the pandemic accelerated and cemented this trend.

Work changes all the time, in millions of little ways. But technology serves as an important disruptive force in our lives, because it is a highly visible change, and also one we can control. We cannot have our company opt out of a pandemic, but we can choose not to implement the latest software update.

How Technologies Lead to Job Transformation

Let's go back to the example of the coal shoveler who was observed by Taylor and his stopwatch. Technology can transform the worker's job in two ways: either by replacing the need for coal or by offering him a more efficient way to do his job.

Let's start with the first type of transformation. Say we figure out how to convert garbage into clean-burning fuel through some miracle technology. Overnight, no one wants coal anymore. Is this guy out of a job? Could be, but probably not. Instead, there's now a lot of demand for someone who can shovel garbage. So the worker goes and gets a job doing that.

Or say that someone invents a new technology that can shovel coal at a much faster speed. But the problem is, the new technology doesn't use hands to operate it but feet, like riding a bicycle. Is the hand-shoveling guy out of a job? Probably not; he just uses his feet all day, pedaling, instead of using his hands to shovel.

These are two simple, and silly, examples, but they illustrate the truth of how technology changes jobs. Instead of automating jobs or replacing them completely, these technological innovations simply transform the nature of work. The modern farmer—to use a real, nonsilly example—looks completely different from what we think of when we think of a stereotypical farmer. Back in the day, farming was a very labor-intensive job, which required high levels of physical labor and many, many workers. Now farming is a much more capital-intensive profession, and most farmers are essentially machine operators.

Part of the reason why technological advances always lead to transformation rather than automation is because technological innovation, on its own, does not lead to productivity. Instead, different business processes, combined with new technologies, are what lead to increased productivity (and, therefore, new and different types of jobs).

When the electric motor first replaced the steam engine, for example, very little actually changed. Factories would have one very large steam engine that powered all the machines within the factory. When an electric engine replaced the steam engine, the new technology was a little bit smaller, a little bit safer, and probably a little more efficient. But it was essentially the same process as before: one big engine, running everything.

Eventually, someone realized that you could put one small engine in all the machines rather than relying on one big engine. This change to engine in every machine allowed factory workers to operate the machines independently of each other and to rearrange the placement of the machines. This technological advancement fundamentally shifted the workflow of the factory, allowing for the creation of a new business process called the "assembly line." It was that innovation of work processes—not technology—that created an increase in productivity. The new process—the assembly line—led to job transformation, creating the need for specific assembly line workers who previously may have been operating the machines connected to the big steam engine.

All of these examples illustrate the four avenues through which disruption via technology can lead to job transformation: outputs, tools, processes, and inputs.

Outputs

In my hypothetical example, I illustrated how a new magic garbage-burning technology transformed the work of a coal shoveler. Well, that silly example has actually happened, with new forms of fuel being discovered or invented many times over the course of human history. When electricity was first harnessed, it completely changed what we produce as an economy—namely, we started to find ways to produce more electricity—and the jobs that came with it. We needed electricians, electrical appliances, repair people for those appliances, and on and on. Technological disruptions can completely alter the composition of our economy and shift our capacity for production and the jobs that come with it.

Tools

Technological changes can also create new tools to use in our work. Electricity allowed us to create lights so we could work later; we developed calculators to use instead of adding machines and telephones to make long-distance calls. Each of these tools created us new jobs—accountants, telephone operators, and so on. Computers and the internet led to emails, websites, and so much more, which also created all the new jobs associated with those technologies. The term "Luddite" actually comes from a group of textile workers in England in the early 1800s who actively destroyed new automated tools for producing fabrics, as they felt that these tools were a threat to their livelihood. Some academics, like Nobel Laureate and MIT economist Daron Acemoglu, have tried to reclaim the story of the Luddites as correct in their decision to smash a technology that did end up costing them their jobs. However, this view does not account for the role of job transformation in a constantly changing and shifting economy.

Processes

Technological advancements can also give us new processes and transform the way we do work through those processes. Technological advancements lead to new, standardized business processes that dictate new types of work.

For example, with the first generation of computers, it was incredibly expensive to start a software company. Doing so required the purchase of massive servers, which were too expensive for any but the largest companies.

Now, however, we can rent out a supercomputer for about $10 an hour. No investment in hardware is necessary.

Cloud computing has made file storage and data transfer so much easier. Companies like Google offer these services for free, in fact. The invention of cloud computing has created a complete shift in our business processes. Even the smallest of businesses, such as sole proprietors, are expected to have a website. Some job applicants even create their own website to have their resume and experience stand out from other applicants. The process of creating a company website as a standard process would have been unthinkable even 30 years ago.

The most obvious example of technology shifting business processes, and the way we do work, is the adoption of high-quality video conferencing software, through Zoom, Google Meet, and Microsoft Teams. These services were available for many years, but few were operating at a seamless level. Once the pandemic hit, everyone was forced to use those technologies at scale, which in turn forced the technologies to improve. Now that we've optimized that technology, we have entered into a different workplace paradigm, where hybrid work or even fully remote work is no longer outside the realm of possibility. People work with other people each day that they've never met outside a video conference call.

Technologies can also help us work together in new and different ways. My company (like many) has a remote workforce, and we leverage our video conferencing software to help build team dynamics and relationships. We create breakout rooms at all-staff meetings where people can participate in icebreakers and other team-building exercises. Our internal Slack platform has a "donut meeting" function, in which it randomly assigns two coworkers to a virtual meeting to just hang out and chat, as you might do in a company kitchen over donuts. (Unfortunately, Slack does not provide the donuts for these meetings.)

Inputs

Finally, technology can change the inputs that we have to our work and, therefore, the work itself. Through technology, we can access—and even create—different types of data that transform the nature of our work.

Like many people, I am trying to get in shape. I use a fitness app that allows me to track what I eat, how much I exercise, how much I sleep, and more. I'm able to input something as simple as "a handful of pistachios" into my app, and it spits out the number of calories contained in that snack. Or I can input that I exercised on a treadmill for 30 minutes, and it will know how many calories I burned.

Without this app, all of these inputs would be useless—or, at least, so difficult to determine that they would be functionally useless. Because of the technology that allows me to more easily track my daily health activities, a completely new industry has transformed personal fitness and the way personal trainers and other exercise professionals interact with their clients.

How Technology Displaces Jobs

When considering the transformation potential of any new technology introduced into the market, we can ask three questions to determine just how much it will automate jobs:

1. How widely will the technology be adopted?
2. How adaptable will workers be in response to this new technology?
3. How flexibly can the work adapt to transformation?

The first question helps us consider how widespread the effects of the technology will become on the nature of work. If a new, innovative technology is released, with a lot of potential to change the way we work, but no one uses it, then its disruptive power will essentially be zero. The question gets at the demand for the new technology: How much do people want the new technology?

Assuming that the technology is widely adopted, then the second question can help us determine how disruptive it will be for workers through the automation of tasks. A technology can be widely adopted, but workers will not be displaced if they can adapt to using the new technology. Instead, with the adoption of the technology, the jobs and nature of their work will transform. The question gets at the supply for labor: How quickly can jobs adapt to the new technology?

The third question is related to the nature of the job and how quickly the job itself can adapt. The flexibility of the work is about the interplay between job crafting and top-down transformation. If the job is itself inflexible and cannot evolve with the new technology, then it is likely to become automated. The question is about the mix of demand for the job and the supply of labor.

For a job to become truly automated, all three questions need to be working against the job. If the technology becomes universally adopted but the labor supply is flexible and the job can transform, then there will not be full automation. If the labor supply isn't flexible but the job is, then the job will transform into something else. If the job can't transform (as in the case of telephone operators) but the labor supply can move into new jobs created by technologies (like secretaries), then those jobs won't be displaced.

The case of John Henry is the classic case of when all three things are working against him. In his story, the demand for the new technology was incredibly high. Everyone wanted a man's labor to be replaced by the faster steam engine. In Henry's case, his labor supply was incredibly inflexible; in economics terms, it was "inelastic"—he could do only one thing, and if that was replaced by technology, he would be out of a job. John Henry couldn't adapt; he could only compete against the machine until he died.

When we talk about disruption and new technologies, what we are most concerned with is the extreme example of John Henry: that our jobs will be replaced by machines. The answer to the third question above was a definite "no" for John Henry. His work was completely inflexible; he couldn't do anything else—and so he not only lost his job but his life. We have similar fears about AI, which I explore in more detail in the next section.

However, we have seen time and again that, even with technologies with incredibly high demand, the labor supply adapts quickly enough that, in fact, automation does not happen and people are able to remain gainfully employed.

Telephone Operators: Displacement That Never Happened

David Deming, the dean of Harvard College, shared the example of telephone operators on his blog, *Forked Lightning*, to illustrate how technologies that would seemingly put people out of work actually can help improve the well-being of those same people.[1]

When the telephone was first introduced, there was no concept of a "telephone number." You could not pick up the phone and call someone directly. Instead, you had to connect to a telephone operator, and you would tell her (telephone operators were almost exclusively women) who you wanted to talk to. She would then use a switchboard to physically connect your call to the person you wanted to speak with.

Telephone operators were a massive segment of the workforce, because of the complexity of the job. In the first few decades of the 1900s, telephone company AT&T was the largest employer in the United States, and the vast majority of its workforce were telephone operators.

However, there was a problem: The job was terrible. Deming highlights that turnover at AT&T at this time was around 40%. As more and more people got phones, the job became even more complex and stressful, because there were just that many more potential connections to make. People expected to pick up the phone and talk to the person they wanted to talk to, as fast as possible. That pressure created terrible working conditions.

Soon the role of telephone operator became automated. Everyone received a telephone number, and the rotary phone made it easy to call that number. The need for telephone operators disappeared almost overnight.

The introduction of telephone numbers was a massive technological disruption among a large segment of the US workforce. So what happened? Were these telephone operators out on the streets, with nothing to do?

Deming cites research that shows that, indeed, certain types of telephone operators were worse off. The older you were, the harder it was for you to find an equally well-paying job.

But the legions of women who were preparing to become telephone operators as they entered the workforce were fine. In fact, they were better than fine. Many became typists and secretaries, and the demand for those occupations skyrocketed as the automation of the telephone made communication more seamless.

The automation of one job—the telephone operator—created a massive demand for another type of job—managing and organizing the large uptick in communication that came from the disruption of automated phone calls, through secretarial work.

That technology did create disruption in our economy, automating some level of work, but it also created new demand for something that didn't exist before.

Case Study: Will AI Take Over Our Jobs?

AI is driving a similar transformation of work as the introduction of telephone numbers did in the early 20th century. AI has offered us the opportunity for massive levels of automation in our lives. With this automation comes fears that no one's job is safe.

However, AI did not come out of nowhere. As a software tool, AI has been evolving over the past several decades to get to the point where it is now. Much of what we thought of as artificial intelligence even just a few years ago is far behind where AI is operating today.

Many people began to see what was possible with AI when IBM introduced a computer that could play chess, named "Deep Blue." Created in the late 1980s, this machine was revolutionary at the time but ultimately was able to complete only one specific task based on a specific set of circumstances (i.e., make moves on a chess board given specific situations in a chess match). AI evolved further and was able to produce IBM's Watson, which was designed to answer questions trained on massive amounts of information, such as encyclopedias and literary works. Watson was able to play the quiz game *Jeopardy!* successfully, defeating some of the greatest champions of all time. But again, this usage of AI was a specific use for a specific situation.

Watson was an early form of the generative AI that we now use through programs like ChatGPT, which is AI software that can use past data (i.e., "memory") to execute and determine outcomes. The software uses these "memory" capabilities to predict the next word in a sentence when delivering an answer to a posed question. Virtual assistants and self-driving cars do the same thing: They look at existing data to make predictions about what is likely to come next, to help someone schedule a meeting or avoid an obstruction in the road.

For all this evolution in AI, though, one thing remains: It is simply a tool to be leveraged. New AI technologies introduced these days may seem like magic, but that magic lasts only until we learn how to use them.

We can use the three questions in the previous section to determine how much we should be worried about AI coming from our jobs.

How Widely Will the Technology Be Adopted?

We can say that AI will be widely adopted, across all areas and levels of our economy. Companies are already beginning to integrate AI into their business processes to help them with data entry, managing appointments, responding to customer requests, generating initial drafts of documents and communications, and much more. Individuals use it in their lives for research, brainstorming, and even answering factual questions that come in day-to-day conversation.

How Adaptable Will Workers Be in Response to This New Technology?

The answer to this question is still unclear. For certain professions, workers may struggle to adapt. Doing so will depend on workers' comfort with technology and overall flexibility. For people like my daughters, who grew up asking digital assistants to complete tasks, using AI will come easy to them.

However, regardless of the comfort of the workforce, it's likely that workers will be quite adaptable to changes driven by AI. As happened to the generation of young women who entered the workforce just as telephone operators were becoming obsolete, there will be new opportunities that can replace the work that does not exist anymore. It's hard to know, exactly, what those opportunities will look like because we are still in the middle of the transformation. But, if history is any guide, any automation through AI will offer new and different ways for employees to complete their tasks.

How Flexibly Can the Work Adapt to Transformation?

Given that AI has become—or will become—ubiquitous, this question is the big one on everyone's minds. The answer, unfortunately, is that it depends. Much will be based on the work's inherent ability to reconfigure in response to AI.

However, for even the jobs that are seemingly the most susceptible to automation, transformation is still possible.

One big potential for AI is self-driving cars and trucks. This technology is already in use in some places and industries and certainly poses a large risk for people employed as drivers. If AI can take over driving a truck across the country, then there is no need for a driver. This job is relatively inflexible. It's not like the job of a coal shoveler who can shovel something else or use more powerful shoveling tools. If you are a driver and no one needs drivers anymore, for anything, then you will likely be out of a job.

The AI-driven transformation of drivers, though, has some parallels to the transformation of telephone operators. Truck driving is a very challenging job. Drivers spend days on the road, away from families, often in dangerous scenarios. Turnover is quite high.

If truck driving became fully autonomous (which is still not a certainty), then while there may be no need for drivers, many other needs will be created: Planning the most efficient routes and timing for deliveries. Overseeing the automated trucks and troubleshooting problems on their routes. Truck repair and maintenance. Or other jobs that we cannot even conceive of right now because we are in the middle of a transformation. The existing capabilities of AI technologies are powerful, but because they rely on past data and experiences, AI programming can never fully reason in completely or even somewhat new situations. Humans, though, can use AI to augment their own reasoning and make decisions more efficiently and productively.

Automated telephone dialing created an entire new infrastructure of communication, which led to new and different tasks. Automated truck driving will, in the same way, also offer truck drivers new and different jobs, some of which may be better paying and more stationary for the former (or potential) truck driver. Potential telephone operators who became secretaries were able to make calls more easily, which freed them up to do more productive things and helped them advance in their career and create a better life for themselves and their families.

AI will certainly automate some *tasks*, but it will never be able to automate full jobs. If you only do one task in your job, potentially you could lose your job, but if you are only doing one thing, repeatedly, every day, you probably do not have a great job. If that one task you do is automated, then there are other tasks out there than need to be done. Looking at AI as a technology that automates *tasks* rather than jobs can help us understand how to best leverage AI for job transformation. AI helps us to complete tasks, in the same way that the better shovel helps us complete the task of shoveling coal more efficiently. AI should be a tool to be leveraged to help us be more productive.

AI—or any nonhuman, machine technology—can never replace our jobs because jobs, as discussed in Chapter 3, require an orchestration of tasks. Machines are very bad at orchestration. Because there is so much involved in the process of categorization, machines cannot easily replicate the combining and coordination of tasks.

Successful orchestration requires a level of deconstruction and understanding of the work being done, at both the level of what needs to be completed and the sequencing of those tasks. No machine could ever grasp that level of understanding because doing so requires context, connections, and constraints. These elements are unavailable to machines because they cannot think.

John Henry's biggest failing was not that he wasn't strong enough. It was that he did not recognize a fundamental truth about technology and job transformation: Humans should not compete with machines on tasks. If a machine is designed for a specific task—hammering steel drill bits, or data entry, or reconciling calendar appointments—it is unlikely a human can compete with that machine, since machines do not need to eat or sleep.

Instead, humans should compete with machines on orchestration and use AI and other technologies like the tools that they are. Machines cannot compete, at any level, on the way work gets done, because they are not human, and they cannot conceive of the way we work together.

But we, as humans, can understand the nature of how we work together, and we can use this understanding to increase productivity. Taxonomies help us categorize the deconstruction of work, the connections between work activities, and how teams collaborate. Taxonomies make work visible and can formalize the system to help our orchestration of work at scale.

The next chapter begins walking us through the process of using taxonomies to do all this—and more.

PART II

How to Build Taxonomies

PART II COVERS the specifics of what a taxonomy actually looks like, how to build one, and what you should do once you have created one. Chapter 5 focuses on the mechanics of creating taxonomies—specifically, how artificial intelligence and large language models can be leveraged for job architecture. Chapter 6 goes deeper into what those concepts look like when applying a jobs-based framework. Chapter 7 offers some best practices for building taxonomies.

5

The Fundamentals of Building a Taxonomy

LET'S BEGIN OUR discussion of how to build a taxonomy by showing an example of a real taxonomy from Revelio Labs. Figure 5.1 shows a simplified taxonomy for "Healthcare Professionals." We sometimes refer to this as a taxonomy tree (for obvious reasons—it looks like a tree). This chapter walk through the basic steps of how to construct such a tree.

You'll see under the "Healthcare Professionals" category six occupational categories, each with its own suboccupations listed underneath. Patient care has six suboccupations: advanced nursing professionals, physicians, general nursing, nursing managers, emergency medical professionals, and healthcare support. Each of those categories contains further subcategories, which contain many different jobs, and each of those jobs contains different compositions of tasks and work activities.

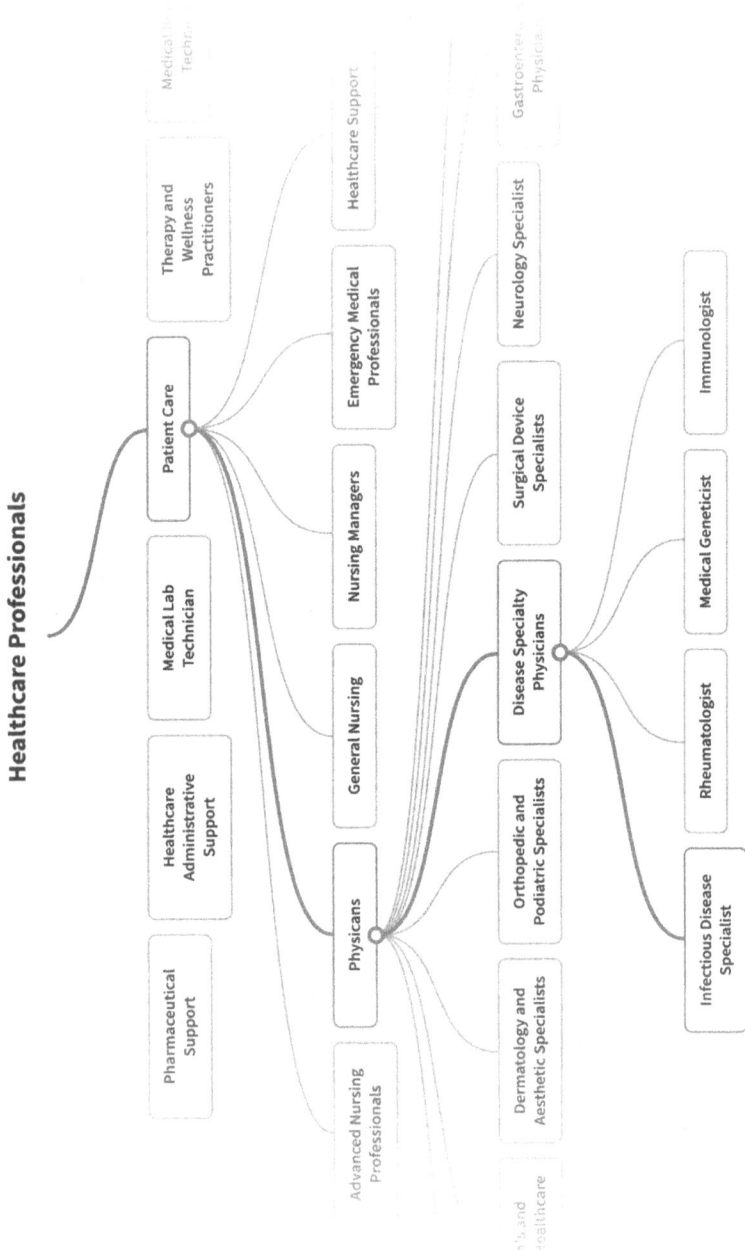

Figure 5.1 Taxonomy tree for "Healthcare Professionals"

In this example, we expand the "physicians" suboccupation category and then again the "disease specialty physicians" category to see what kinds of jobs make up this occupation. Underneath "disease specialty physicians," we see four different job titles: infectious disease specialist, rheumatologist, medical geneticist, and immunologist. All of these jobs deal with different types of doctors who specialize in treating different diseases. Infectious disease specialists deal with viral, bacterial, and fungal infections, whereas rheumatologists treat autoimmune and inflammatory diseases. Medical geneticists support patients with genetic diseases, and immunologists work on diseases connected to the immune system, like allergies or autoimmune disorders.

Taxonomies must be flexible because of the inherent nature of categorization. Think about how we talk about animals. My daughter understands the difference between cats and dogs but also the difference between "big dogs" and "little dogs." For her, this distinction is sufficient. But if you brought your dog to a dog park, full of other dogs and their owners, distinguishing "big dogs" from "little dogs" would get confusing quickly. You'd want to be able to talk to the other people at the park about their Chihuahua or pug or black Lab or Labradoodle. In this way, "dogs" is a flexible category that can adapt based on the needs of the "user" (a child versus an adult at a dog park).

When a taxonomy tree is in place, it can become the unit of analysis for how to think about and manage the workforce of your company or the entire human capital system. You can compare across these taxonomies to understand differences across divisions, benchmark pay against competitors, and do workforce planning to identify gaps in your existing employee capacity.

The taxonomy tree itself is simple, and its power comes from its simplicity. But getting to that simple layout is anything but simple. You cannot just draw boxes around your existing job titles and then stack them based on your best guess of how they connect together. That kind of organization leads to the house of cards described in Chapter 1.

Instead, to create a functioning taxonomy, you must go through a robust and technical process of putting your workforce data through a large language model (LLM). LLMs are pattern-recognition tools trained on massive amounts of text. The LLM's pattern recognition power allows it to see the phrase "on the same page" used over and over and then predict that the word following "on the same" . . . will likely be "page."

Most people interface with LLMs via their predictive, generative function. (ChatGPT is the most famous example.) However, when it comes to building taxonomies, we do not use LLMs for their text-generating ability. Instead, we use them to encode information and create what are called "embeddings." *Embeddings* are what help categorize the important elements of a workforce taxonomy, such as job titles, skills, and responsibilities.

We harness the encoding power of LLMs to create taxonomies through these six steps:

1. Data collection
2. Embeddings and transformers
3. Clustering and slicing
4. Labeling
5. Inference
6. Versioning

Data Collection

The first step in constructing a taxonomy through an LLM is to bring together a massive amount of data. In our taxonomy catalog at Revelio, we draw on an extensive array of data sources, including online profiles, resumes, and job postings. This diversity of datasets ensures a comprehensive view of the activities and skills associated with each role.

We collect data through two sources: public data, which come from public sources, such as online professional profile, job postings, or other job sites where job descriptions and other job-related information are posted; and partner data integration, which gathers data in collaboration with our clients for industry- or company-specific data.

This raw text can include job titles, associated activities, and skills from professional profiles, job postings, statements of work for consultants, or internal descriptions of jobs.

To create a successful taxonomy, you need to be able to use sufficient raw text data pulled from these data sources. The process requires a large sample size of data to create more precise models. If there isn't enough data for the model to use, then the data will become noisy and not an accurate depiction of the real world.

Luckily, "pretrained" models come with the data built in. These open-source LLMs like Llama or ModernBERT already have processed a lot of data.

You can use these pretrained models outright, but the result will be very generic. These models have been developed with a lot of data and a lot of nuance to be usable for all kinds of applications beyond workforce data. The data will not have the appropriate level of nuance that you are looking for and, therefore, will not be very useful for the eventual analysis of your workforce.

If you want to get into organization specifics, you will need something that is more specifically trained to your own data. Putting 10,000 of your own job positions, for example, into the LLM will help you gain more nuance in your taxonomy. Doing this will help you tease out the nuances within your company. For example, a data product analyst and a data business analyst may seem like similar positions to everyone else, but they may have huge distinctions for your own company.

Embeddings and Transformers

LLMs use the data to create what are called "embeddings," sometimes referred to as "vectors." *Embeddings* essentially take a word and assign it a random string of hundreds of numbers to translate the word's meaning into a mathematical concept. A simplified example would be: *page* = [1.5, –0.4, 7.2, 19.6, 3.1, 20.2]. As the model gets trained and grows and develops, the random initializations of values change so more similar things are closer to each other, essentially helping the model make sense of all of the words it contains.

So, in the case of "*on the same page*," each word—*on*, *the*, *same*, and *page*—would receive a string of numbers, completely randomly, so the program can assign it an "embedded" meaning within the model and allow for machine learning activities that can analyze and understand the data more effectively.

Essentially, these embeddings allow LLMs to find the patterns between words that the models would not be able to understand without those assigned numbers. These models have no inherent concept of what a "page" is, but they do understand it in relation to the terms around the concept. "Page" may be seen as close to or similar to "paper" or "book" or "notebook," for example. But by embedding these words, through the assignment of random numbers, the model can predict how frequently "page" appears in relation to other words, including words that may not actually be related to its embedding, such as "same" or "on." A lot of data is required to create this level of pattern recognition, which is why we need millions of lines of text to "teach" an LLM.

"Transformers" are a related concept to embeddings that help LLMs function. The development of transformers was essential for software to develop natural language processing, or NLP, which has led to the conversational tone we can now experience with various AI interfaces. (The "T" in "ChatGPT" stands for "Transformer.")

Embeddings can help predict words in a sentence, but *transformers* assign weights to words through analyzing how words relate to each other, across sentences and millions of lines of text. Essentially, a transformer can help the models to recognize (again using the example of "on the same page") that "on" and "the" are less important words in this particular phrase than "same" or "page." It can determine that "same" and "page" contain more meaning than "on" or "the." This ability allows transformers to better understand patterns and offer more complex analysis of data. Transformers give LLMs better predictive power. They are able to understand that if someone says "We're so alike. I love that we think on the same ___," the sentence is more likely to end with "wavelength" than "page."

Transformers can help LLMs make much more complex determinations of language and writing. If someone says "Hold on. I don't think we're on the same ___," transformers can understand the context of the preceding words and know that the next word will be "page" rather than "team," or "side," or something more ridiculous, like "watermelon." A bad LLM would essentially just be a Mad Libs, the old game where kids place random words into blanks in sentences.

Once all of these embeddings and transformers are assigned, the data can be categorized and manipulated. Each word will be assigned a spot in the model in relation to other words. Words that are close together frequently are determined to have similar meanings and then placed at closer "distances" within the model. This placement within the model is how we can begin to form relationships between concepts such as job titles. The LLM tells us that certain jobs, such as social media manager and communications associate, are quite similar, and other jobs, such as staff attorney and city bus driver, are very different. These distances can help us to start to build effective, workable taxonomies.

Clustering and Slicing

Let's use the metaphor of a pizza with olives to illustrate how we proceed in developing our taxonomy. The pizza is the LLM, and the olive is a piece of data—an embedding—on that pizza. For this example, let's assume pizza is a linear, two-dimensional space, and the olives are data points on space. Because we are working with workforce data, the olive would be a particular occupation. (See Figure 5.2.)

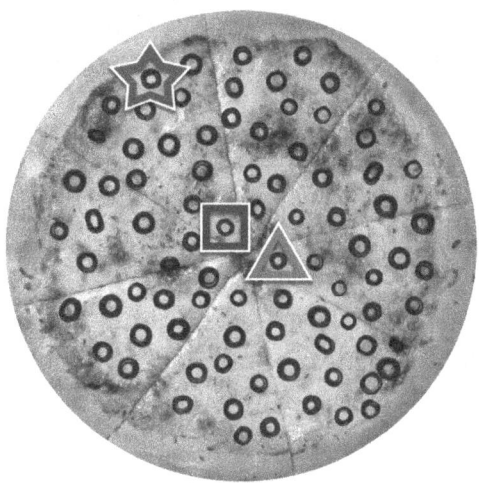

Figure 5.2 Olives on a pizza: New Africa / Shutterstock.com

We can now figure out the connections among the different olives, and cluster them together, based on how they relate to each other. We find these connections, essentially, based on how similar their component parts are; if two different occupations have similar activities, then they should be clustered together. Once we cluster them together, we can build the taxonomy tree from the data, like the one depicted in Figure 5.1.

Clustering comes by "slicing" our pizza into different sections. By slicing the pizza, we group our olives together in similar categories. We want to make sure we slice this pizza in the traditional way and don't cut it into squares, because in our model, we are going to have embeddings that spread out from the center of the pizza toward the crust. Two olives may be similar, but one may be closer to the middle and one may be closer to the crust. By slicing the pizza, we're able to capture each of these spread-out olives and categorize all those similar jobs together.

For example, a somewhat generic job that kind of does everything will be closer to the center of the pizza. (Generic data always fall closer to the center of the model because it has higher connections to other data in the model.) A generic job might be a project manager—someone who completes tasks like "communicating with stakeholders" or "ensuring tasks are completed in a timely manner." There's not much specificity to that description, so it would be closer to the middle of the pizza because it has a lot of connections to other jobs. These are the olives that are in the square and circle in Figure 5.2.

More specific jobs, such as diagnostic radiologist, would be very far from the center of the pizza, almost near the crust. (This is the starred olive in Figure 5.2.) These jobs have very little in common with the other jobs that are closer to the center, so they have to be farther out in their own spot on the pizza, nearer to the crust.

This concept works not just for job data but for any kind of data. You can plot out various movies across an LLM pizza to see how they cluster together. You'll see groupings of genres like sci-fi or rom-coms or superhero movies, or even more specifics like Marvel movies from the 2010s or original Disney animation from the 1940s. All of these are just points in space, where you can then create slices to identify clusters and develop taxonomies.

Now, why would it matter then if we were to use cookie cutters to punch out sections of this scatterplot pizza? Would it be so bad to group the specific jobs together and the general jobs together? Why not put the circle olive and the square olive in Figure 5.2 together, separate from the star?

Because grouping the olives in this way assumes that we have good, clean, precise data. If we can be certain that every piece of data within the pizza is accurate, then sure, we can use the cookie cutter method. (There are still some reasons not to do that, even with accurate data, but I won't go into that here.)

But unfortunately, our pizza isn't perfect. We are operating in the real world, not in the world of models and assumptions, and our data can be quite messy. In most cases, when something ends up in the middle of the pizza, it's not because it's a true generalist job, but because it's a lazily written or poorly articulated job description. The job is actually a real job with specificity, but the data we have to represent the job as an olive on the LLM pizza is poorly written or perhaps just a copy of a job description that was first written years ago.

This kind of data is noisy, which is sometimes lovingly referred to as "garbage." You know the adage: Garbage in, garbage out. I am sure you have seen some of these garbage job descriptions—they are so vague and generic that it's almost impossible to understand what the job actually entails.

When a model does not have good data, which happens frequently, the olives that represent the job descriptions get pushed to the center of the pizza. This clustering at the center is why slicing is important: It helps to mitigate the challenges with a lack of good data. Clustering puts the garbage data into slices, which helps to identify categories because while the data might not be perfect, there is a little signal in the noise. The olive is likely being pulled toward the crust—toward more specificity—and that direction is probably the right one. Slicing up the categories from the crust down to the center helps to cut out the signal from the noise of the messy reality of the data. We can place the star and square olives from Figure 5.2 in the same slice—or cluster—to make a more appropriate grouping.

Consider two different categories of jobs and what happens when you use slicing versus the cookie cutter approach. Two olives that are closer to the center of the pizza would be more generic titles, like handyman and school nurse. More specific titles, such as maintenance technician and licensed practical nurse, would be closer to the crust. These are basically the same jobs with different titles. One set is more generic; one is more specific. We want school nurse grouped with licensed practical nurse, and handyman with maintenance technician. We can do that by using slices to categorize the jobs.

Once you get these slices, you can move on to the next steps of labeling your categories, inferring where new data belongs when it comes in, and, finally, versioning the taxonomy over time.

Labeling

Once you have your data and you've cut up your pizza into slices, what comes next?

Well, you could be done. You could build a taxonomy from those slices (which, at this point, are also called "clusters") and leave it at that. But the problem is that, while the model understands those slices and the categories contained within, they hold no meaning for your average human.

Once everything is sliced up, each of the categories will have an ID that is associated with the taxonomy, but these are just random numbers assigned by the model. You'll get results like Cluster ID 135; Cluster ID 567; Cluster ID 897. These have meaning within the model, but when you take that data and present an analysis to senior managers, for example, they might have a hard time following the recommendations, because Cluster IDs mean nothing to them.

These generic IDs produced by the model are the reason we have to label our slices in order to build taxonomies that are useful for organizations. Without labels, the output from the LLMs won't do much good in the real world. It will make sense to a machine, and to the extent we have machine-run processes, we could use the machine-produced IDs. However, we do not have fully machine-run processes yet, so our clusters must be labeled in ways that are both machine readable and human readable. We want to be able to use the insights that AI has offered us.

Naming our cluster slices may seem like a straightforward process on the surface, but it actually can be quite complex.

Usually, when we have a cluster of job titles, we just pick the most common one to label that cluster, because it typically serves as an overarching job title. But that does not always work. Consider this cluster of jobs to see why: physical therapist; speech therapist; occupational therapist. We can't use that simplified convention with this cluster, because physical therapist is not actually an overarching job category that includes speech or occupational therapists. Although those jobs are related, distinct differences exist between the jobs within that cluster.

What we want this category to be called is something along the lines of therapeutic occupations, but that label does not likely exist anywhere within the data that has trained our model. As humans, we can extrapolate that category title, but the machine does not. We can manually create this title if we want to do so, but doing that at scale, across thousands of categories, can be quite time-consuming.

Luckily, ChatGPT and other generative language models can do this work for us. These models can take the clusters we have created and assign them titles based on their own pretrained understanding of the world. Doing this allows the process of labeling to happen much quicker and more efficiently.

But relying on AI for labeling can get complicated. Generative AI also gets tripped up sometimes with labeling, so the process is not as simple as asking "Hey, ChatGPT, what would you call this cluster of 50 job titles?" The model will offer up the simplest answer, which probably will be the most generic one and therefore will overlap with other job titles.

Let's say you have two of the pizza slices next to each other, and they both have jobs related to software engineering. But there is enough distinction between the two that you want them to be separate clusters. So you ask ChatGPT to label the first one, and it spits out "software engineer." Fair enough. You do the same thing for the second one: "software engineer."

Obviously, you cannot have two categories with the same title at the same level. Instead, a better cluster label might be "backend engineer" because the software that the occupation works on is C++ and other backend technologies. The other label then might turn into "frontend engineer," highlighting the difference between the two and making them more usable to categorize for the taxonomy.

You create these labels by showing the generative AI what is *not* in the category. You say: "What would you label a category of jobs that includes these but does not include these?" And the ones to *not* include are the job titles that are around the boundary of the cluster—the olives that are close to the edge of the slice. That way, you can avoid the generic, meaningless category labels.

(Note: This process of labeling was developed by the Anthropic team, the makers of the generative AI Claude.)[1]

Inference

All right, now you have your slices, you have them labeled, and you can spend your days working with all of your neat and orderly taxonomies. Your job is done!

Not so fast. The real test of your taxonomy has not even begun. That's because your categories are only as good as their ability to absorb new information. Our world is not static, and new jobs and skills and activities will arise from the changing nature of work. Your taxonomy will be useful only if it can handle this new information. This process is called "inference," meaning that your model can infer where to place new jobs as they arise within the workforce.

Let's say someone is hiring for a hypothetical job that no one has ever had before—"Reporting Product Associate for Telecom." This is new data, a new olive that needs to find a home on your pizza slices.

All machine learning models distinguish between training and inference. *Training* is when the model takes existing data and, assuming the data are good and not garbage, turns that data into something that can make sense of the world. Training is, essentially, the model trying to reverse-engineer the world.

Inference is when that model is running and considering what new developments, in the real world, mean for its model representation of the world. It tries to figure out, or at least give a best guess, as to where this new olive should fall on the pizza.

How does the model do this? Well, if this new job title called reporting product associate for telecom pops up, it can look for similar job titles. Maybe it has something to do with product associate? Or telecom associate? Or maybe product reporter? Analyzing all of these similar titles, at the scale of millions of pieces of data, can help the model determine where this job title fits on the pizza.

If someone (or a group of someones) is currently in this new role, the model can take a look at their previous positions and use that data to help it identify where the role belongs. If many people in that role previously held the role of telecommunications reporting analyst, it's probably a good bet that this new role has something to do with the old role. As time goes on and as more data are added to the model, the inferences will improve.

Or let's take a different example: a very ambiguous title. Let's say someone has the title "associate." We would want to infer a different occupation depending on whether they work at a law firm or an investment bank. "Product manager" can also be ambiguous, even within the same industry. The job might mean an engineering lead at Facebook or a client success representative at Google. Unfortunately, this is the case with many jobs and is why we have so much noise in the data and, therefore, olives that cluster around the center of our LLM pizza.

Inference, at its core, is the process of determining what jobs are the same or similar. Relying on job titles alone will not be enough. Instead, we must consider the composition of activities and tasks. Inference estimates the true distribution of activities, then classifies them to the right occupation.

The issue of inference is quite a difficult problem for LLMs (or, actually, for the human programmers who create and use the LLMs) because algorithms are data hungry. To train a model well, you need billions of sentences and forms of data. This is why companies like OpenAI are seeking out new sources of data, after blowing through all existing data sources on the internet, which also opens up issues of trademark and plagiarism (but that is a topic for another book). They, and other AI developers, must be very concerned with how informationally efficient their models are.

One way to deal with this is a brute-force method: Just use as much data as you can. You don't have to choose between looking at similar job titles or previous roles when identifying a new title; you can just use it all. You can also throw in skills, activities, and the connections an employee may have to other employees in similar roles on LinkedIn. Why not? This approach works well with common titles—associate, project manager—but not with the more specific ones. No matter how much data you have, there are always going to be some jobs with imperfect categorization.

So far I've been talking about a model in two dimensions: The olives exist on a plane in space, and that plane is a pizza. But you can add different dimensions to your model to get more information that can be used for inferences.

Just as adding a third dimension to a flat pizza will give it depth—turning it into a pizza ball—more dimensions in a model give more nuances to the data. This concept is hard to visualize, because we only see in three dimensions (and experience four with time). But most models have way more than that; ChatGPT has thousands.

In practical terms, if you have two dimensions, then your model can distinguish between two different parameters, such as if the work is what we'd consider "blue collar" or "white collar," for example. You can add in another dimension to get more specifics, such as if the job is technical or not. Or if it's full time or part time. And on and on.

Of course, you may be thinking: Why not just pile on the dimensions? Wouldn't you want as many as possible?

The problem is the curse of dimensionality. When you add more and more dimensions, you get a lot more noise as well. Things get more complex, and the model can "overfit" your data, creating complexity where there is none. That's because along with all of these dimensions in your data comes a lot more empty space. Things that are actually quite "close" to each other, in terms of categorization, appear far apart in the model. The pizza gets stretched out and twisted around, and it's harder to create slices of accurate categories.

This curse leads to a trade-off: nuance for simplicity. Adding more dimensions offers more nuance but also can create unnecessary complexity. When designing an LLM that can complete accurate inferences, you have to decide how much nuance is needed while not adding so much that the model becomes unusable. The right level depends on what you are trying to do. ChatGPT is a very powerful model, which is why it has so many dimensions. Having so many dimensions produces a lot of nuance but also requires a lot of data.

Versioning

Now that we understand what data is required, slicing (clustering) the pizza, and how new olives find their way to the pizza through inference, there's one last concept to consider: versioning. *Versioning* is the updating of a model while ensuring that the new model can be effectively incorporated into business processes.

Versioning is a relatively simple concept in our modern technological era, because we experience it all the time. It's the reason we buy new cell phones or have to update our software periodically. As things evolve and change, we not only need to adapt to the new information, but we must also update the foundations of the model that allow it to take in that data.

If you swiped open one of the first-generation iPhones today, you would probably laugh at its simplicity. To be honest, I don't even remember what those phones looked like. But I remember the first time I used one—I was amazed. Now it would seem antiquated and outdated.

However, when it comes to taxonomies, versioning is much more complicated. Because there are many users of a taxonomy, any updates require backward compatibility. *Backward compatibility* means that users of an old version need to map to the latest versions, requiring all versions to be maintained at all times and the development of crosswalks between versions. For an iPhone, the versioning happens directly on the phone, and users start to use the new or updated operating system.

This versioning happens for two main reasons. The first is the most straightforward: Things are wrong. Software always has bugs in the system that need to be fixed. If you ever look at the periodic updates to your cell phone's operating system, you will see a list of minor changes that were discovered through user operations.

The other reason for versioning is for improvements. The interface can improve; new features can be introduced; data security can be strengthened. All of this comes with the territory of software development. Sometimes people don't like the changes (how frustrating is it whenever our phones update their software with new interfaces?), but the goal of versioning is continuous improvement.

In the case of our job taxonomies, versioning helps to recognize the emergent nature of the workforce. Emergence captures the idea of new job titles—like "reporting product associate for telecom"—but also the shifting nature of work itself. Because jobs are always changing, the fundamentals of a model should be analyzed and considered periodically to reflect those changes. Would you trust a model built in the 1990s to accurately infer the state of work today? I wouldn't.

I've discussed the many issues with the labels from O*NET, but one of its primary limitations is that while the data may update periodically (new job titles are defined and categorized), the updates from government data are lagged and limited, meaning that they do not keep up with the times. New versions come out in the same way that dictionary updates are released periodically. In the age of AI, that just doesn't work anymore. By creating taxonomies through LLMs, we can create adaptable, flexible categories that update their understanding of work in a way that is responsive to the changing dynamics of the workforce.

Now that we understand the fundamentals of building a taxonomy, we can consider what this process looks like specifically for the workforce and human resources.

6

Creating a Complete Workforce Taxonomy

CHAPTER 5 LAID THE foundation for how to develop a taxonomy tree—of anything from basic words in a sentence to jobs—through embeddings within an LLM. This book, however, is about a specific type of taxonomy: workforce taxonomies. Everything in the previous chapter applies to taxonomies broadly, but more specific elements of categorization must be developed to create a functioning workforce taxonomy.

To create a successful and workable taxonomy for workforce data, you should develop taxonomies across three different areas: activities, roles (synonymous with "jobs"), and skills. I introduced the connections between these concepts in Chapter 1, in Figure 1.1. The workforce taxonomy elements all interact with each other, with activities serving as the components of a job and skills serving as attributes of the people who fill those jobs. Only when you develop a taxonomy for each of these areas can you have a true understanding of your workforce needs and capacities.

Activity, Role, and Skill Taxonomies

Activity taxonomies are developed from the description of activities within and across job profiles and resumes. The data contained within the profiles and resumes are processed through an LLM that results in an embedding for each job title, categorized through the "slicing" process described in Chapter 5, and then labeled. The activities are created as the fundamental building blocks of work, categorized absent their association with a title.

For example, an activity taxonomy may contain the work tasks of "public speaking" and "press release writing." These activities may be in a similar category of "communication," but they may not be found in similar roles. For example, a CEO role may be built off the activity of "public speaking" but may not be required to write press releases. A PR associate may spend their days writing press releases but be too junior to have public speaking responsibilities.

From these clusters of activities, we can form representations of jobs. Each job can be represented as a collection of activities. For example, a job could consist of 20% public speaking, 20% writing, and 60% project management. This distribution of activities would form the job. If another job, regardless of the title, has the same distribution of activities, we would say they are effectively the same job or role.

Role taxonomies take these distributions of activities for each job and combine them to form clusters. These clusters of roles are called "occupations." The clustering is developed in the same way as the activities, but with slightly different data. Like activity taxonomies, role taxonomies use job profiles and resumes, but the data inputs are the responsibilities sections of job postings as well as the bullet points on resumes. Through the inference process, after the initial taxonomy is created, we develop the roles not by accepting job titles as they are written but by creating some approximation of the role or occupation through an analysis of similar activities. We do not want to assume that any new job title assigned to a role is the "true" title, given how much variation workplaces have for describing roles. For example, just because someone at a company labels a job posting as a product manager does not mean it is materially similar to another company's product manager. What that company calls product manager could be closer to a software developer at most companies.

Skill taxonomies are the final taxonomy component for a complete workforce taxonomy. The skill taxonomy uses the activity taxonomy to inform its categorization. Instead of clustering the words associated with the skills, we cluster the skills associated with a similar set of associated activities—that is, skills that are required to do a certain task or activity are grouped together. If someone lists a skill of "Microsoft Excel" on their resume as well as "Microsoft PowerPoint," we might cluster those together in a skill of "Microsoft Professional Suite." These skills can be grouped at whatever level of depth we need, and we can see what skills are similar to each other. For example, "Microsoft PowerPoint" might be similar to the skill of "Canva," another presentation software.

The next sections describe subtle nuances on how to train your LLM on these three different aspects of a workforce.

Activity Categorization

To create an activity taxonomy, we use the process developed in Chapter 5: data input, assessment of similarity and distance, hierarchical categorization, and labeling. The data, in the case of activities, are activity descriptions (basically, sentences from job profiles and resumes). Through transformers, they are placed in the model, clustered together based on similarities, and labeled appropriately. Activities are much more difficult to categorize than job titles or skills because every sentence to describe an activity is unique. Skills, for example, have a lot of overlaps, in the way that two people (or 200 or two million) may have "Microsoft Office" as a listed skill. It's unlikely, however, that two people have two identical activity descriptions on their resumes, even if those activities are similar or identical in their execution.

For example, two people may complete the activity of "filing documents," but one job description may describe this activity as "Ensuring the appropriate storage of company files" and another may list it as "Maintaining document accessibility through record keeping."

Once the model moves into inference, another complexity arises because of the nature of the data itself. Activity data from job postings (such as the responsibilities section) differs in fundamental ways from the activity data from profiles (such as bullet points on resumes). On postings, the descriptors are typically aspirational and written by hiring managers or recruiters. On profiles, they're backward looking and written by employees. So there may be some language differences, in that an employee won't necessarily write the activity but the outcome of the activity (i.e., "I helped the company grow by 5x") or something else entirely. For example, on my LinkedIn page, in the description of my responsibilities, I actually don't have anything at all related to my day-to-day job responsibilities. Instead I have a description of my company.

We deal with these inconsistencies in the data by reducing the focus on the activities that don't have sufficient overlap. So language like "resulting in $20m in revenue growth" would be treated as an uncommon outlier and would likely not show up in the final taxonomy of activities.

Another way we deal with the complexity inherent in our data is using something called "topic modeling." The most well-known topic model is LDA (latent Dirichlet allocation). If you are attempting to analyze a set of news articles, for example, LDA can find similar groups of sentences or paragraphs within those articles that all relate to the same concepts. Entertainment articles will have more sentences related to movies and TV shows, sports articles will have more articles related to players and scores, articles about the weather will have sentences related to temperature, and so on. With text categorized by theme, you can label each group of articles and tag each article to the topics that it contains so that you can search for articles with the same topic. So sports articles are labeled with the topic of "sports," entertainment articles are labeled as "arts" or "entertainment," and the like.

We take the same approach to labeling with activities, but the topics are instead the description of the tasks completed via the activity. Instead of broad topics ("filing documents"), we construct the taxonomy with enough specificity to produce descriptive labels such as "filing 1099 forms," "setting up semiconductor equipment," or "managing payroll vendor relationships," for example.

After using the LDA process, the model measures similarity between the workforce activities and assesses how closely related two activities are to each other. For example, "manages a team" would be closer to "helps organize projects" than to "operates heavy machinery." Measuring the distance in the model between the activities can help to create the different levels of hierarchy, similar to how we can drill down from healthcare professionals all the way to infectious disease specialist. (See the taxonomy example in Chapter 5, Figure 5.1.) An activity taxonomy could be "Management" and include the component taxonomies of "Manages a team" and "Organizes projects."

Role (Occupation) Categorization

When the model is in its initial training phase, categorizing roles follows the standard process already described: The model takes the job titles and assigns them embeddings, and we are able to categorize and label those titles.

Once the model is in use and moves into inference, we do not include only distinct job titles as data inputs for the roles; nor do we look only at the job title itself. Instead, we capture more data, including the entire online profile or resume of someone filling that role or the job posting of the role. By looking at the activities contained within that more comprehensive information, we can get key insights into the type of work being performed, which is then automatically aggregated across matching titles to create activity compositions for every role.

For example, if we wanted to categorize the role or occupation (again, these terms are synonymous) of someone with a "Project Manager" title, we would use not only the job title as an input but also everything associated with someone who holds that title: the resume; previous jobs; the skills listed on any public profile, like LinkedIn; and any internal job descriptions associated with that role that a company might have. When we run the model, the LLM would find that all the information associated with this "Project Manager" title implies that it is instead closer to a "Program Manager" role. If we were to rely just on job titles alone, the LLM would have less information to rely on and would create much noisier data.

Role titles with similar activity compositions naturally share similar functional work and responsibilities, which means similar roles will be closer together on the LLM pizza and will be categorized together. For instance, a data scientist and a data engineer share many of the same activities (writing code, managing databases, etc.), while a physician performs entirely different work; consequently, a data scientist is closer to a data engineer than to a physician within the model.

Once we have these activity compositions, we can then begin to create the hierarchical clustering—essentially moving up from the infectious disease specialist occupation to the healthcare professionals category from Chapter 5 in Figure 5.1. At each step of this categorization—going from infectious disease specialist to disease specialty physicians to physicians to patient care and finally to healthcare professionals—a decision must be made on how to categorize things together. The choice for categorization usually happens because of the level of "distance" between the different points in the model. But we also need to consider how many observations are in each category.

Consider what would happen if you had 1,000 roles in a model and about 900 of them are close to each other. Then you have another 90 that are close, and then a final category of 10 that are close. Having this grouping distribution would be very ineffective—saying that 90% of the roles are in one category and the rest are split across two. Instead, the model automatically groups the closest together as they relate to the size of the group, grouping the smaller categories together first and ending with the larger ones, so that we don't have such large distributions. This approach to grouping also helps deal with the issue of high levels of noise within the data. Maybe these roles are all similar, or it could be that there's a lot of ambiguity in positions and the roles should be farther away from each other in the model.

This example of 1,000 roles is completely hypothetical, but it is close to what we find when we complete these models. Most jobs are close together within a model, with outliers here and there. By considering the distance between these points in the model as well as the sum total of the roles in the category, we can create a more usable taxonomy. Through this approach we are able to, for example, explore nuanced differences between different types of medical science liaisons at a pharmaceutical company while simultaneously standardizing the company's IT department into key functional areas.

To optimize our clustering, we use something called a "silhouette score," which is basically the ratio of between-cluster variance and within-cluster variance. We want clusters that are far from each other and where the elements inside each cluster are close to each other. We want clusters that are distinct from each other (far away) but groupings inside that are similar. Grouping data in this way is a perfectly sensible objective for a clustering algorithm, except that it doesn't consider the size of the elements (number of jobs) within each cluster. If there is a job with a lot of data points in one cluster—such as a job that a lot of people have, like project associate or something similar—it's more useful to split the cluster. Or if there are a handful of clusters that are close to each other and all the jobs inside them are tiny—such as a job that not many people have, like rare book librarian—it's probably useful to cluster them together or let them glom onto bigger surrounding clusters.

Skill Categorization

Skill taxonomies are developed using the same basic patterns just described: data input, assessment of similarity and distance, hierarchical categorization, and labeling. Because of the nature of skills, less uniformity is required within the clustering, as compared to roles and activities. Skills are categorized at a much more specific level, in a much more niche way, because jobs that are more similar may have different skills associated with them.

For example, data warehouse engineer and data lake engineer are two different roles that are mostly the same in function. Each is responsible for managing and maintaining data, but the data are different. This difference in the types of data managed is what makes their jobs distinct: data warehouse engineers work with structured data whereas data lake engineers work with unstructured data.

Although the activities are quite similar, the skills differ in nuanced ways. Data lake engineers use very different software and different coding requirements from data warehouse engineers. There are differences in skill requirements between the two jobs, but the activities (and therefore the roles) are mostly the same: manipulating and storing data. The job itself is similar but done in different ways.

Although the skills will be more specialized, they can be labeled and categorized using the same process as the other role and activity taxonomies. We all have real, tangible skills that we use each day; we just have a hard time communicating those skills in concrete terms. What people list as their skills—"communication," "data analysis," and "Microsoft Excel"—are representations of the true skills they have. The underlying skill being performed might be "sharing information to help work be completed," "understanding data outputs to make operational decisions," and "using the software tool Microsoft Excel to perform a variety of necessary tasks."

However, if a group of these skills is similar enough and has similar enough connections—"writing" with "writing speeches" with "blog post writing"—then they can be grouped together, categorized, and labeled with something that more closely resembles a skill, such as "executive communication support" or something similar. In this way, the model can capture the latent meaning of the skill that exists in the world and place it into a taxonomy for more effective analysis.

The way we talk about and write down our skills creates some challenges with the categorization toward a usable taxonomy. For example, the closeness of skills to each other within a model is complicated by their simplicity. You probably would never see both "database" or "databases" listed as a skill on someone's resume, because those things mean the same thing and listing both would be redundant, just as you would never list both "Excel" and "Microsoft Excel."

Nonetheless, one person's resume may list "database" as a skill and another's might list "databases." Because these skills would literally never co-occur with each other on a resume, the model will think they are completely different things, even though they are literally the same thing.

Here's how we deal with this dilemma: We look at how skills co-occur, or how close they are within the model, to similar occupations and activities. We can see that PR professionals have a lot of similar communications skills, and we see that, for example, drafting a press release co-occurs frequently with writing skills. By looking at skills in this way—based on their intersection with the work being done—we can create a taxonomy of skills that is more reflective of what capabilities the skills unlock. If we instead use the strict co-occurrence level of analysis, we would have a taxonomy of skills that placed Excel and Microsoft Excel about as far away from each other as they could be, which would render the taxonomy completely useless.

Relying on skills as a foundation of job architecture ignores the fact that jobs are not made up of skills but are made up of activities. Both jobs and skills should always be embedded by the activities they are associated with. The "skill-based" approach to work misses this important nuance in the process of categorizing work. There is now a huge push for companies to hire employees based on a consideration of skills, but this push is mostly coming from the vendor community. Adoption has been slow precisely because the approach does not make sense with respect to work output.

Companies hire people into jobs to get stuff done. If there's a push to hire based on skills, that's fine, but only if those skills can be connected to activities that align with the work getting done. If that connection can't be made, then the skill-based approach will have a hard time solidifying across industries. The work being completed—the activities—is the unit of analysis, not the skills themselves. Skills should instead be seen through the work they unlock.

Seeing skills as connected to activities allows the distance between two skills within the model to reflect their functional similarity. For example, "Python programming" is likely to be closer to "data analysis" than to "customer relationship management," given their shared context in data-focused roles. An activity-based lens can also capture both fine-grained relationships (e.g., differentiating between programming languages used for web development versus data science) and broader patterns (e.g., clustering soft skills like "team leadership" and "effective communication").

Once the skill taxonomy is complete, we can then map each role to it, allowing for precise analysis of the most critical skills or competencies required within an organization. This mapping also enables deeper insights into skill gaps, emerging trends, and areas for targeted workforce development initiatives.

With these three different taxonomies—activities, roles, and skills—in place, we can begin to see how they interact with each other, influence each other, and support broader decision-making within an organization. Their connections allow for detailed analysis of the most common work being performed at an organization and gives management and other decision-makers a better understanding of how work is being performed.

7

The Right Way to Construct Taxonomies

Now that we understand how to build a taxonomy, and before we move to the practical implications, I want to summarize and pull out some of the major takeaways from the previous chapters and provide a few criteria for how you should be thinking about taxonomies. These criteria are relevant not only for your company or organization but also on a broader scale for the widespread adoption of taxonomies as a useful tool for our economy—because all this work to better categorize our labor and our jobs will not be useful if, well, it's not useful.

Just like the example in Chapter 3 about the tomato is sometimes a vegetable and sometimes a fruit, depending on how we use it, taxonomies can help us only if we can use them to better understand and manage a workforce. As should be clear by now, a lot of the work of taxonomies is quite technical and complicated; nonetheless, you should never lose sight of the ultimate goal of implementing taxonomic structures into your organization or across an industry: arriving at a better understanding of the work being done, leading to increased productivity and improved employee well-being.

I have found, through my work as a data scientist and running Revelio Labs, that there are seven characteristics of a useful taxonomy: organized, hierarchically flexible, adaptable, auditable, able to evolve, mappable, and (somewhat) universal. This chapter walks through these characteristics and helps you understand the degree to which a taxonomy framework will work for your organization.

Organized

Taxonomies should be organized with a thoughtful structure that is grounded in the nature of work. The taxonomy should be developed based on the definitions covered in Chapter 1: Categories of jobs should be created with a fundamental understanding that jobs are made up of activities and that occupations are a cluster of jobs. Many people do not have this basic understanding and therefore create a set of taxonomies that cannot help them manage their workforce.

For example, right now, there is a large amount of interest in what is called "skill-based work." This approach has a simple promise: By considering skills that employees need to complete their jobs, employers can more efficiently execute on work tasks and support employees to respond to a rapidly changing work landscape. As new technologies push the boundaries of how we do our work, it's appealing to think that deconstructing jobs into certain skills and supporting employees to "skill up" in those areas can help companies stay ahead of the rapid pace of change.

Unfortunately, that's not how work works.

The skill-based approach to deconstructing work makes a fundamental error in assuming that jobs are collections of skills. This is not true. Skills are not the building blocks of jobs; instead they are attributes of people to help them excel at their jobs. Someone can have a collection of skills that are well suited for a particular job, but, ultimately, jobs are not made up of skills. As covered in Chapter 1, jobs are made up of work activities.

A good taxonomy for human capital must be organized around work activities rather than skills. Skills are useful only to the extent that they help complete work activities, but activities are what lead directly to business outcomes or outputs. These outcomes or outputs are what drive a business forward, determining its ultimate success or failure.

Let's say an organization did rely on a skill-based approach to its taxonomies, not on an activity-based one. What would happen? Well, the company would probably not completely fall apart, but it would also not be as efficient or productive with its workforce. The focus would be on the experience of the employee, not on the work getting done. Ultimately, that focus would lead to a disconnect between the company's desired results and the experience of employees. Instead, an activity-based approach can help employees understand how they can best contribute to the company, given their own interests and constraints, and the company can determine how to best orchestrate the work being done in service of its goals.

Most taxonomies used by firms do not meet this test of "organized." Many taxonomies currently in use conflate a skill with an activity with an occupation. For example, "blockchain" could be listed as a skill, a job, and an activity to be completed. Specifically, when it comes to skill-based taxonomies, or taxonomies that rely on skills as the central unit of work, there can be a lot of confusion over what is and isn't a skill,[1] which reduces trust in the model and discourages employees and practitioners from using it.

Hierarchically Flexible

A taxonomy should also be hierarchically flexible to be useful for an organization. Essentially, a taxonomy should contain several clustered layers within the tree, so users can choose the level of specificity that matches their needs. Doing so will help users learn more about the different levels of the categorization.

Flexible taxonomies are just as useful for high-level analysis as they are for in-depth analysis. A finance department might want to operate with only 10 categories. Talent acquisition, however, may need a lot more; maybe it won't be satisfied even with 1,000 categories. That's because the work of talent acquisition is much more dependent on the specifics of the taxonomies. Someone working in talent acquisition needs to know as much as possible to hire the best people for the job. A category of engineer isn't enough for a hiring team, because that is way too broad. Is it a Java integration engineer? Technical architect? DevOps engineer?

But if you were to present a finance team with a set of 1,000 categories in a taxonomy, they would probably smile at you, thank you for the impressive analysis, and never look at the taxonomy again.

Most companies do not have flexible taxonomies. All taxonomies have some element of flexibility, because without some level of drilling down and drilling up, a taxonomy would be too cumbersome to use. But most taxonomies do not contain enough granularity to be functional. There might be enough specificity for a compensation benchmarking initiative, for example, but not nearly enough for someone in the talent acquisition department trying to hire new employees.

Adaptable

A taxonomy needs to be adaptable to the different contexts across companies and industries. The taxonomy structure should recognize that there is not a standard set of occupations in the world, with all companies maintaining predetermined types of jobs. Each company has its own needs, and a taxonomy should be able to adapt to the different contexts of companies. There is always a way to go deeper within a particular occupation, depending on the work and needs of a company.

For example, a small company may have only one lawyer on staff as general counsel. That company does not need to go deep on its categorization of lawyer within the workflow of the organization's operations.

However, a law firm, obviously, would hire many different kinds of lawyers, all with different work activities and responsibilities. The firm's HR department would need to have a deeper understanding of the tasks assigned to lawyer, and the resulting jobs that come from those work tasks, than the company with just one person hired as a lawyer. In fact, the law firm would likely have many job titles under the occupation of lawyer, such as law clerk, associate attorney, partner, managing attorney, and so on, whereas the company with one lawyer may just have the position of lawyer or staff counsel.

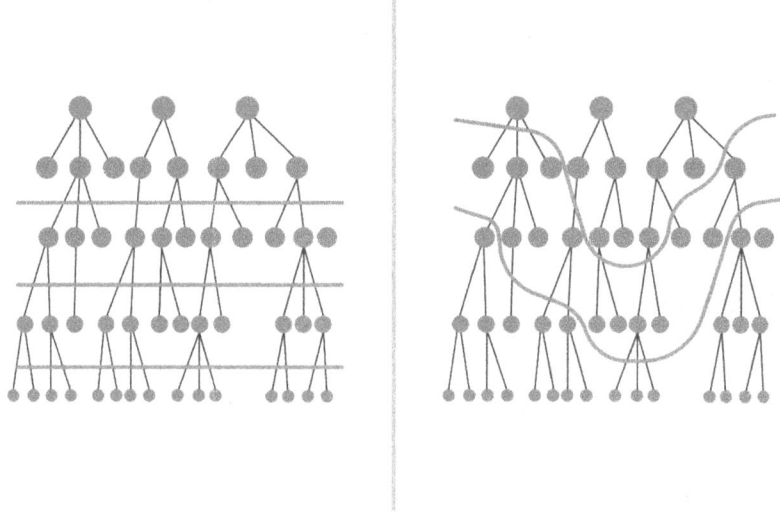

Figure 7.1 Unadaptable versus adaptable hierarchies

The difference between these hierarchies is illustrated in Figure 7.1. On the left, you see a hierarchy that cannot adapt, with clear lines across jobs (the dots). Each line represents a level of granularity within the taxonomy. The higher the line, the broader the categorization, and the lower the line, the more granular the categorization. The left depicts a universal segmentation for a one-size-fits-all taxonomy. On the right, the squiggly lines allow for a segmentation that goes deeper in one part of the tree and stays broad in the other. These squiggly lines are a more ragged cut on the tree; they allow us to use the same tree that's on the left, but the cuts produce more custom segmentations for different companies and industries.

A lack of adaptability is the issue with the federal O*NET system that comprehensively lists out any and all jobs with specificity. An unadaptable, O*NET-like hierarchy is on the left—a standard cut across the tree of job categories. What companies want is a taxonomy tree on the right, which removes what they don't care about and includes only what they do care about. Adaptability and customizability can help the hierarchy be deep where it's appropriate to be deep and broad where it's useful to be broad.

Adaptability is one area in which current taxonomies excel. Almost every company with a taxonomy has done the work to create a bespoke system to meet its needs. Unfortunately, this adaptability comes at the expense of universality, which is discussed in detail later in the chapter. The unique nature of each constructed taxonomy means that companies cannot compare across their industries. (Sometimes taxonomies cannot even be compared within companies, as taxonomies may be used only within certain departments or functions.)

Many firms think that you must sacrifice standardization for specificity when constructing taxonomies. However, due to our ability to create the ragged cuts shown in Figure 7.1, we do not have to make this trade-off. This false trade-off leads to companies spending large amounts of money on consulting firms that come in and build taxonomies from scratch rather than leveraging more adaptable taxonomy structures. Once the work of the company evolves, the specific taxonomy created is no longer relevant and becomes outdated quickly.

Auditable

One thing you do not want your taxonomy to be is a black box. You can spend time working on establishing the different elements of the taxonomy—the work activities, the job categories, the occupations—but if you cannot trace the connections between those things, then the taxonomy will not be useful. Auditing the taxonomy—being able to explain the decisions made within the taxonomy and why it is set up the way it is—helps to illustrate the connections and embeds its usefulness across a company.

An element of auditability is particularly necessary with taxonomies for larger organizations that have more complex structures. Without clear reasoning behind the setup, you are left saying "Trust me, all of this works together." This type of reasoning is not a way to build trust. If, instead, you can show your logic behind the setup, you can support the broader adoption of the system.

An auditable taxonomy can show why things happen the way they do. Understanding the connections between the parts allows for easy fixes when something goes wrong.

For example, at some point with one of our taxonomies, we had an issue in which software engineers were being tagged with contractor and home builder skill sets. This level of tagging was odd, of course, and so we looked into it. What we found was that there was a skill set within software development called "Rust," which is a relatively common programming language. Of course, there is another meaning of the word "rust"—the rust from metal that a contractor or home builder might have to deal with. The LLM did not understand the difference between these two skill sets—the Rust programming and the removal of rust—and so made a nonsensical connection in the data. When we discovered this error, we fine-tuned the embeddings so that they would be able to detect when different units have the same name and take context into account so that issues like this are dealt with automatically. If we didn't have a system that was easily auditable, we would not have been able to do this fine-tuning and make a systematic improvement to the model.

The ability to audit a taxonomy is a critical part of an effective taxonomy because it will help the taxonomy be sustained within an organization. You do not want the people who originally created the taxonomy to have to explain the connections over and over again. The system should be bigger than one group of people. The only way to create a taxonomy that doesn't become obsolete after a few years—as so many do—is through an intentional process that can be replicated. Then, even if the team who built the taxonomy leaves the company, the taxonomy will still be understood and remain useful.

Many existing taxonomies fail the test of auditability. Taxonomies are created based on assumptions determined by a small team of experts (either internally for an organization or externally through contracted consulting firms). These assumptions typically are hard to explain, are not grounded in sound logic, or both. The process becomes a black box without much transparency, leading to mistrust in the system and lower levels of adoption within the firm.

Even when taxonomy designers have the best intentions, auditability can be a challenge. After I helped create a skill taxonomy at IBM, we published a paper that described our methodology in an attempt at transparency.[2] However, the paper presented an incredible technical explanation that no one who was not a data scientist would understand. No one could realistically check our work. We were describing the black box a little bit, but not in a way that was functionally useful. Our colleagues at IBM still had to take our word for it that the taxonomy was sound.

Able to Evolve

A strong taxonomy also needs to be able to evolve to the changing economic landscape. This characteristic is related to but different from the characteristics of flexibility and adaptability. The ability to evolve focuses on the taxonomy's ability to absorb new types of skills and job characteristics as they enter the market. For example, social media manager was not a job that existed before 2010 or so but has become an essential role for many companies in the last decade and a half.

When I started my career, the job of data scientist had not yet been formalized into job architectures. I was working at a hedge fund, essentially doing the work of a data scientist, but no one knew what that meant yet. My job, instead, was quantitative strategist.

As I became aware of a new field of data science, I began to understand what that type of job could do for a company. Data scientists are less focused on statistical analysis and more focused on creating recommendations with data that help companies make decisions. I was doing these activities in my job as a quant strategist, but the work was more akin to a statistician than a data scientist who offered recommendations and direction for a company.

I don't fault my old employer for not labeling my job correctly, because the term "data scientist" was so new. The company caught on quickly and evolved to bring in data scientists to support its operations. But if it hadn't, the workforce would have been stuck in the wrong boxes, working on activities that were not as productive as they could be.

Taxonomies that evolve have benefits not only from the company side but from the labor side as well. After a university rebranded its statistics department as a "data science" program, enrollment for the next year tripled. The professors were teaching a lot of the same material, but once they shifted their offering slightly to match the markets, students (and future workers) were able to benefit from clearer and updated categorization.

If a taxonomy remains the same over a long period of time, it likely is not useful. Imagine a system used within a company that still has a place for typist or even telephone operator.

Almost no companies have taxonomies that can evolve because they do not have taxonomies that rely on LLMs. Without LLMs, taxonomy categories become static and obsolete as work transforms, which, as discussed, is happening constantly. The only way to have an evolvable taxonomy not dependent on LLMs would be to have HR managers or other practitioners who are managing the taxonomy stay on top of all the ways work transforms across the workforce. This task would be incredibly difficult, to the point of impossibility. Instead, taxonomies are updated in a more manual way whenever they become outdated enough to require an update—a burdensome and costly exercise.

Mappable

A taxonomy should be easy to map to. As new jobs grow and develop, their place within the taxonomy should be found easily—the new jobs can be placed within the existing taxonomy, "mapping" onto it. You can take whatever new job that was created, such as a social media manager, and find it a place within the hierarchy. For example, it is likely that a social media manager would be connected to a communications section or marketing section.

The current O*NET structure does not have a mappable characteristic. There is no way to understand where new job titles belong within the existing structure. When a new job function like social media management comes along, someone has to do the work from scratch to understand the work activities contained within that job and how it could relate to the existing data within the system. There is no easy way to directly map that new role into the definitional structure of O*NET.

The same is true for the taxonomy of most companies. Because these taxonomies are highly bespoke, emerging roles or occupations cannot be easily mapped to them. If a company decides to go into a new direction—maybe adding a new product line or service—then it would have to start completely from scratch with a new taxonomy rather than merely mapping the new roles to the existing taxonomy based on the work activities that must be completed.

When new roles appear that don't fit into existing categories, they usually are classified within the "other" field in the taxonomy or workforce data system. The "other" category allows for a free text entry, creating a completely new category tied to nothing else within the taxonomy. The data in these "other" fields—the newly emerging jobs—are siloed away and unable to be fully integrated into the taxonomy. As more and more jobs become "other," the taxonomy's usefulness completely breaks down.

(Somewhat) Universal

The mappability of a taxonomy is especially important as we think about how to scale taxonomies across industries. A taxonomy can't be truly useful unless it has some level of universality that applies across companies and organizations so that we can compare trends not just within a company, or between similar companies, but between industries. This characteristic allows for an entire market analysis, not just an analysis on company data, just as how Bloomberg Terminals can be leveraged to better understand the capital markets.

There is, however, a trade-off between the universality of a taxonomy and the flexibility just described. We want taxonomies to be flexible so we can customize them to specific organizations, but not so customizable that there is not a universal nature to them that allows for easy comparison between companies.

If there are 25 million companies in the world, we do not want to have to create a taxonomy for each of them, because that would not be useful. If each company had its own unique taxonomy for its workforce, it couldn't perform benchmarks on things like salaries or make other comparisons with peers. Not only that, prospective job applicants would have to navigate 25 million different ways to think about work. Each company would have its own language and perspective on jobs.

But one taxonomy for those 25 million companies would also be unmanageable. This is essentially the problem with O*NET right now: It has attempted to create a completely universal framework, and in doing so, its taxonomies are not useful to companies because they cannot be customized easily.

Instead, we need something in the middle that allows for flexibility but also universality, because companies and organizations within the same industries likely operate more or less the same as each other. There's no need to create a unique taxonomy system for each company, because a sales associate in one retail company is probably doing similar work to a sales associate in another retail company.

Most taxonomies in existence right now do not meet most, much less all, of the seven characteristics of a useful taxonomy. The goal is to create a system that meets each category, because if not, the positive elements of each can be sacrificed and the full benefits of taxonomies will not accrue to organizations and the economy as a whole. Without each of these elements, the taxonomies will be less functional and harder to use, limiting their influence on the different stakeholders in our economy. These specific benefits are the focus of Part III.

PART III

Using Taxonomies

THIS PART WALKS through the challenges faced by a variety of stakeholders in the field of workforce intelligence and explains how taxonomies can offer a solution. Chapter 8 focuses on job seekers, Chapter 9 focuses on investors, and Chapter 10 focuses on organizational leaders.

8

How Taxonomies Support Employees and Job Seekers

EVEN THOUGH SHE is only three, my daughter is already starting to build her own taxonomy of jobs. In her world, there are only about five: doctor, teacher, firefighter, zookeeper, and astronaut. Certainly these are all great jobs, but there is not a lot of consistency between them.

I do not know if my daughter will one day hold any of these jobs, but she is already beginning to think about what her occupation might be, which is not surprising. Many people start to form their opinions of jobs quite young, and exposure to certain jobs at an early age can affect their eventual career choices.

Because these professions are the building blocks of my daughter's understanding of work, she filters everything through this lens. She says my wife is a "feelings doctor" (she's a therapist) and she says I'm a "doctor of work." In her mind, there is a category of "doctor" and we both fit into that category because we help people solve specific problems. My wife helps "fix" people's feelings, making them feel better, and I help companies "fix" their workforce problems.

In this way, every job is focused on problem solving. Children inherently understand this. My daughter and I play a game in which she gets to pick an occupation and act it out. Let's say she's a doctor. I'll knock on the door and say, "Ouch! I fell down the stairs and I have bruises all over my leg!" She'll pretend to take my temperature, give me an ice pack and a bandage, and tell me to get rest.

When I was growing up, I had only a vague notion of what my parents did. I knew that they had some kind of office job. As I got older, I learned more about what their occupations. I finally understood that my dad was a kind of a data scientist for his time. I did not figure this out until I was well into my own career. He was essentially doing the equivalent of the work I would eventually do. Would I have benefited from knowing more about that kind of job, even from a very early age? Would my career have been different?

Maybe not, but it could have been helpful to have more information about what my dad did, especially since I ended up doing something so similar. Instead of knowing about the career paths of a limited set of professions, what if I (or my daughter) was exposed to a number of different potential career paths?

I am now experiencing a similar dynamic through teaching at NYU Stern. The students in my class mostly think that they will end up in one of three occupations: investment banker, consultant, or accountant. Obviously, there are caveats to this observation and granted, this is a business school, but I know from experience that there are way more jobs out there for business students than just those three. My students just don't have enough context for what other jobs really look like or how nonfinance jobs could realistically fit into their career.

This lack of full information about jobs leaves us with a limited set of choices in our career path. It contributes to children going into their parents' profession or the network of a young person influencing what type of job they end up with early in their career. If you have ever been to any kind of job training or career development seminar, you'll hear the advice that networking is so important to secure your next role. That's because what we are exposed to—and have connections to—gets us our first, or next, job.

While the importance of networks and exposure to certain jobs will never change, I would argue that the large emphasis placed on these factors shows just how broken our job market is. Instead of relying on good information for our jobs, we instead must rely on who we know to find our way to jobs or, worse, on our limited knowledge of what kinds of jobs are out there.

This lack of information is the biggest challenge that employees and job seekers have as they attempt to secure employment and ultimately build their careers. Taxonomies can help solve this challenge, offering a full picture of all the jobs in a market. If taxonomies were used regularly and consistently across organizations, and were made public, anyone would be able to explore any type of job and go as deep as possible to understand the different components of that job. No matter their background, where they are from, or their work history, they could learn, almost instantaneously, most of what they need to know about any job.

Low Information Limits Career Potential

What we do for our work is tremendously important. It's a huge decision, but we have little to no information to help inform us about how to make it. Most of our decision-making is based on what kinds of jobs we are exposed to, like my daughter's job role-playing game expanded out across our lives.

If we had perfect information about what jobs are and what activities are required within these jobs, we would be able to create better matches between employees and employers. Instead, we are relying on anecdotal evidence to dictate who might be a good fit for a job or not. If you grow up spending your time at a country club where you meet all kinds of different hedge fund managers, it's more likely that you will go into a career in finance. If you instead have a more working-class upbringing and everyone you know has parents who did not go to college, then you are less likely to go to college and find a higher-paying job associated with that credential.[1]

Certainly there is no dearth of information about jobs out there. Just ask anyone at a cocktail party or social event about their job and I am sure they could happily talk for hours about what they do each and every day for a living. (Whether you would want to hear all the details is another question.)

This information, however, is mostly held in the minds of the individuals who do the work, leading to an information mismatch between employers and job seekers. Sometimes the information is codified and shared in books (like this one), in classes, or through professional development opportunities. If you don't run into a certain type of employee at a party and happen to ask them about their work, it's unlikely this information will be transferred from them to you. You might have a vague sense of what a corporate accountant does, for example, but unless you know one or have spoken to one at length about their work, it's unlikely that you will know enough to know if that's the right job for you.

Consequences of Low Information for Employees and Job Seekers

The lack of good information about jobs has implications for our entire economy. Capitalist tenets are based on the exchange of good information, and without this exchange, we can never have a truly efficient market. Meritocracy is dependent on full competition, which we cannot achieve if there are certain people in certain jobs or on career tracks because of where they were born or their exposure in life.

A lack of information about the full scope of work activities leads to all kinds of problems for job seekers. It hurts not only companies but their prospective employees as well. If applicants do not know the specific details of what kind of job they are applying for, or if the job position is vague and open-ended, they may end up in a job they are not suited for or do not want to do. Just like companies, employees are flying blind, and we all suffer.

Informational issues cause breakdowns within the job market, limiting the potential for employees to succeed in their careers and companies to fully maximize the productivity of their employees. These breakdowns occur in three places: applying for jobs, career development, and job transformation.

Applying for Jobs

When you apply for a job, you need to know what that job is and what completing the tasks associated with the job entails. If there's confusion around what the job actually will be, job seekers are worse off. Employers will also have a hard time sourcing the right candidates. I have seen dozens of examples of job seekers applying to data scientist jobs only to find out the actual work is querying data and producing dashboards, which would be better labeled as business intelligence analyst.

Most of us have been in the position where we are applying for a job that we think is one thing, but, through the interview process, we learn it's something completely different. We think it's for a product development role, but it turns out to be more of a project management role. Worse, you may even get into a job, start doing the work, and find out that something completely different is expected of you.

This inconsistency in job expectations leads to a tremendous amount of inefficiency. Hiring someone can cost a company three to four times the annual salary.[2] Instead of applying to jobs well matched to our experience, interests, and skills, we must send out dozens if not hundreds of resumes to different companies. Recruiters sift through these resumes, hoping to find a potential good match, only to end up learning during the interview process that job applicants inflated their resumes or are not good fits for the job, because the job posting wasn't clear.

Taxonomies, by offering more structured information, can support a more mathematical and precise pairing of applicant and jobs, creating better alignment. It's unlikely that we will ever be in a market where employee and employer are matched automatically—there will always be a human element—but we certainly can operate at a much higher rate of efficiency than we are operating now.

Taxonomies can also, in certain cases, offer specific insight into the hiring practices of companies. Job seekers can see which companies post a lot of positions as well as how quickly different organizations fill open positions. Revelio has also been able to identify what we've called "ghost jobs," in which recruiters ghost applicants, ignoring anyone who has applied while the job posting remains online. This ghosting can be due to a hiring slowdown as a result of economic uncertainty within the company.[3] Data of these types can help better prepare applicants throughout the hiring process.

Career Development

Many firms claim to offer job placement services, especially after layoffs, but these services rarely help former employees find new jobs with a level of efficiency. Networking then becomes the default advice for anyone looking for a job, because absent good and standard information, the only answer is to talk to as many people as possible.

This challenge is almost identical to the one regarding applying for jobs, just extended over a longer time horizon. If we are all fumbling around, trying to do our best to find the best employer or the best employee, career development becomes almost impossible. It's like trying to navigate a map with one eye closed and no depth perception.

With a clear taxonomy for jobs, we can make a more standard path forward with our jobs. We can build one job on top of the other in a standard way. If careers take detours, as they often do, we can see a clear line through them all, even if the line is zigzag. If someone begins a career as a lawyer but then goes into psychotherapy, we may see that this individual had strong observational skills that were consistent throughout both phases of her career.

Job Transformation

Even when employees find themselves in a job, perhaps a job they like and are good at, they still can't escape from the challenges of a low-information market. As jobs transform, employees usually transform with them. They become skilled in different areas or learn how to complete different tasks. Maybe the job isn't what someone signed up for, but as the job changes, the employee changes with it. Maybe someone is hired as a data analyst, but as the work continues and the company grows, the employee realizes that what she is doing is more the work of a business intelligence (BI) engineer, which is more about business performance.

Maybe the person also likes these unexpected responsibilities but has no sense of how the job should be done effectively or how much they should be compensated. If the employee is OK with this changing responsibility, this might not be a problem. In fact, it may be a welcome change if the employee is seeking out new and different responsibilities.

What is a problem, though, is when the employer does not recognize this change in scope and does not change the structure of the job appropriately. The person who is actually a BI engineer could still be slotted as a data analyst and managed accordingly. She might not have access to the right kind of information or work with the right kind of people. Most important, she might not be receiving the same pay as a BI engineer doing the exact same work. The employer has no incentive to increase the pay for workers who are operating at a higher or differently valued level, unless employees have full (or better) information on what they could or should be making at another company.

Taxonomies can offer employees significant exposure into the changing nature of work, as they adapt to new information. By benchmarking salaries, they can also help to ensure that all employees are receiving equitable salaries.

Taxonomies Create Standards

Taxonomies solve the low-information problem by creating a standard for jobs. They offer up curated and collated information that can level the playing field for employees and job seekers.

If people are interested in a military career but are intimidated by the idea of being frontline soldiers, they could click into a military taxonomy, for example, and see that there could still be thousands of jobs to choose from. They would see that the military has an HR segment, which includes the occupation of payroll specialist, and that there is a job titled benefits and workforce analyst. Not only that, but when exploring a specific job, they will be able to understand all the skills associated with the job, including required activities and associated salaries.

In this way, taxonomies become "maps" for a career. They lay out the terrain, show you what's out there, and give you as much information as possible on the different components of a career. Taxonomies are not only a research tool but also somewhat of a choose-your-own-adventure mechanism to help people figure out the different paths to where job seekers would like to be with their careers. Job seekers won't use taxonomies to understand granular data at the level of an employer but instead to research and explore potential career paths.

Realistically, creating a comprehensive taxonomy of the labor market will not solve overnight issues of social inequality or allow teenagers to find their dream job with a few clicks of a button. Career development is a complicated process, and while taxonomies can offer a map, the map alone won't get you there.

Instead, taxonomies should be seen as the foundation of a new wave of thinking around jobs and careers. Just as employers began to understand the potential of the internet in the 1980s, we can now begin to see the benefits of what taxonomies will offer once they are widely adopted.

9

How Taxonomies Can Help Investors

BEFORE BUYING A used car, it's always best to take that car to a reputable mechanic and have it checked out, just to make sure that the car is still roadworthy. Let's say you go to the mechanic, drop off the car, and the mechanic immediately gets into the car, drives around the block as fast as he can, and then returns it to you, saying "Yep, the car goes fast, so it's in good shape."

You probably would find a different mechanic, wouldn't you?

When investment firms look into potential companies for investment, their assessment tools are more or less no different from a mechanic checking only the speedometer on a car to see whether it can go fast. While these firms spend a lot of time assessing qualitative information, most of what they analyze, in terms of tangible data, is a company's performance—if it's growing, what its valuation is, if it made a profit, how much, and over how long of a period. If a company is growing at a rapid rate, then that can be seen as one indicator of a valuable investment.

But we all know fast cars can crash. Consider the crypto exchange FTX. The company was growing at a tremendous rate—its valuation peaked in early 2022 at around $32 billion, with a growth rate of about 25% in just four months and about $1 billion in annual revenue.

Of course, we all know what happened to that company: It crashed and burned. If investors had looked underneath the hood more closely, they would have seen tremendous challenges, including outright fraud, that would have thrown up huge warning signs. No one would have wanted to invest in that car.

If we want a true picture of the health of a company, we need a broader standard than the profit- and revenue-based performance metrics investors use today to assess whether a company would make a good investment. Right now there are no standards for comparison, except for general accounting principles, which are more about compliance than forward-looking performance.

Fortunately, though, we can understand this problem better, and fix it, because we know what is under the hood of a company: its employees, who can be analyzed by using taxonomies.

Taxonomies Expose a Company's Health

I do not want to imply that if we had robust and functioning human capital taxonomies, investors would have been able to expose FTX for the fraud that it was earlier. Much of what led to FTX's downfall was actual financial mismanagement and had more to do with the company's accounting of its funds rather than operational mismanagement.

However, I do know that an analysis of a workforce can help predict and understand company behavior and future performance. There is nothing a company does that does not have some effect on its workforce. From those changes in the workforce, we can better understand the strategy, direction, and health of a company. By leveraging taxonomies, investors can better understand companies and make smarter decisions about their capital. I have seen it multiple times through my work with Revelio.

Through our analysis of the workforce changes in the tech industry, for example, we were able to detect a shift in Meta's strategy on virtual reality. You may remember when Mark Zuckerberg introduced the idea of the Metaverse in 2021, which would be a virtual reality or augmented reality space that represented the "next chapter of the internet." The idea was that everyone would experience the internet using some form of virtual reality (VR) glasses, and instead of engaging through a screen, we'd "live" in the internet, interacting with things as if the Metaverse was a real space, not a screen-based interface. Zuckerberg thought it was so critical to the future of Facebook that he changed the parent company name to Meta as a symbolic turn after many years of hiring VR engineers.

After about a year, though, it was clear that the pivot was not delivering the expected returns. It was reported that after about $1.3 billion in investment, one of the premier Metaverse products had only 38 daily active users.[1] Soon Meta was shifting away its investment from the Metaverse, with which it shared a name and into things it determined to be more profitable, like AI.

This wasted time and money by Meta was obviously not an encouraging sign for investors. If there had been some kind of signal that Meta was pivoting away from virtual or augmented reality, investors may have made a different decision with their capital, especially if they felt that VR was a viable product or business model.

Those investors who followed the Revelio data analysis did see that signal. We saw, in the months leading up to its pivot, that Meta was significantly shifting its workforce away from augmented and virtual reality and toward other areas. We saw a large spike in new job postings that mentioned virtual reality around the time of the Metaverse announcement in 2021, but then a gradual decline from there. Crucially, other companies were still investing in virtual reality at higher rates than Meta, although those investments were dropping too. The difference signaled a shift in Meta outside the market trends.

We also saw that the company with the highest rates of VR investment was Accenture, but its job postings concentrated more on design-focused skills than Meta, whose postings emphasized research and product development. This analysis implied that Accenture was not looking to conduct groundbreaking research but perhaps was hoping to leverage existing tools to help its clients adapt and operate in the metaverse. We determined that Accenture was following Meta's lead, hoping that VR would become a widespread technology that it could help clients implement. Meta was the one developing the technology, supposedly, but our data showed that it was, in fact, not as committed as Zuckerberg's announcement would have made it seem. Figure 9.1 illustrates the change in VR-related job postings over time.

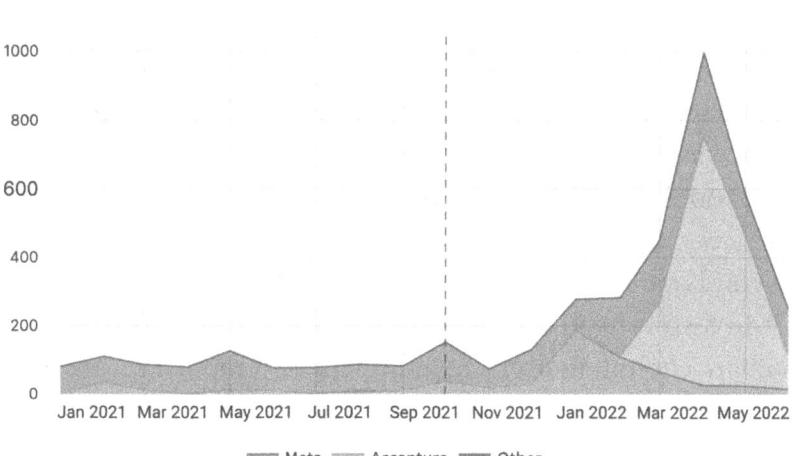

Figure 9.1   New job postings from Meta and Accenture mentioning virtual reality

We shared these findings with *Bloomberg*, which began to work on the story, including reaching out to Meta representatives to comment. Meta, of course, denied that any such shift was occurring. The company did not want to admit the failure of a signature investment, which would have implications for shareholders and investors. Meta threatened to contest the article,[2] deny the findings, and cast doubt on our methodology unless we took down the data reporting.

This made us nervous, of course. We did not want to face the ire of one of the world's largest companies. We redid our analysis, tried making different sets of assumptions about how Meta might be categorizing its VR roles, but the result ended up the same each time. We decided to not back down and stuck by our analysis. It was a somewhat risky move—angering one of the world's largest companies—but it paid off. A few weeks later, Meta announced its shift away from virtual reality, and, in 2024, it shuttered its main VR operations with a pivot to AI.

The data on Meta's VR hiring—powered by taxonomies—opened up the company's hood and looked into its actual operations. Our research was able to get at the true signal of the company's health—its employees—and figured out who Meta was hiring and why. It's one thing to say a company will focus on something, and even announce dollar amounts of resources invested into it, but it's a completely different thing to build out teams and hire real people to get work done.

Investors need taxonomies to analyze companies because human capital matters to companies. Employees are the ones who are completing the work of a company, and shifts in those resources will reflect shifts in a company. These human capital decisions are complicated and are indicative of major changes within companies—why a company is set up in certain places, why it expands into different markets, why it hires certain individuals. If a company wants to sell to a new market, it may set up shop overseas. If it wants to invest in a new area, it will hire people to execute on that work. If it is pivoting away from something, hires in that area will go down. There is nothing that a company does that doesn't somehow manifest itself through its workforce. Any major decision a company makes, or strategic direction it takes, will show up in the hiring of new employees or shifts in workforce. Taxonomies can support an understanding of these changes and the business decisions behind them.

Taxonomies Offer Standards to Eliminate the Tower of Babel

What would it take to get these kinds of data into the hands of every investor? One of the easiest answers to that question is: transparency. With better disclosure of human capital, we will have greater access to data and the insights that comes from them, like our determination of Meta's shift.

Right now there are clear rules and regulations around capital disclosures that help investor decisions. These are the 10-K annual report and 10-Q quarterly reports that all public companies must release to disclose their financial information and capital structure. There are no equally strict requirements for human capital, however.

Every few years or so, there is a push for more transparent human capital disclosures. Sometimes there's some movement on the issue, but usually the policy lands in some form of voluntary disclosure. Currently companies are required to report on various aspects of total number of full-time employees, employee types, turnover rates, and similar metrics, but these requirements have not reached the level required of capital disclosures.

Unfortunately, even with expectations around transparency, little can be learned because there is no way to compare the data that companies release. Transparency is not enough. Instead, we need clear standards so that all the data can talk to each other.

Think about it this way: Even if there was mandatory reporting on job hiring, the reported data would be mostly meaningless outside the context of that one company. If Meta says that about 75% of its workforce is employed as engineers, for example, what does that actually tell us? What kind of engineers are they? What work do they do each day? And, more important, how does that level of employment of the specific type of engineers compare to other companies? Is it the same? Is it different? Has it changed much over the years?

Without standards, we end up with a Tower of Babel situation: Each company's data are speaking a different language. There's no way to know whether a "sales" position in one company is fundamentally the same thing as a "sales" position in another company.

Take, for example, the position of an economist. I myself am an economist. But when I introduce myself as such, no one knows what that means. It's ambiguous. Even so, my company hires many economists. So do major companies like IBM and Amazon. Amazon, in particular, is well known for hiring a lot of economists.

However, all of these positions are completely different across companies. At IBM, economists all work on macro-level reports, such as how the geopolitical situation in China will affect mainframe computing exports. These economists are basically collecting and analyzing trends that would affect the business and sharing those trends with the relevant staff. This job might be more similar to a reporter than anything else, or some kind of industry analyst.

At my company, economists basically fill a hybrid role of data science consultant and client success manager, in which they take the data from our products and help companies understand what these data mean. In this way, the economists are client-facing, almost like customer service representatives. But they also take that data and write articles for our newsletter about trends—similar to the IBM economist focused on trends, but at a micro level, or maybe even to a marketer.

Amazon, however, hires economists to do three different things: forecasting, testing out new business policies, and assessing market structure. The forecasters have backgrounds in macro and finance, time series analysis, and support analyses that consider coming trends. The business policy roles are basically applied statisticians, using data to solve micro business problems. Those who assess market structure use different modeling designs to create pricing schemes and other things related to the online market to support business growth. In hiring these types of roles, Amazon is essentially using a data-driven approach to the company's business practices, helping to maximize decision making in a number of ways. Currently Amazon hires more economists than any organization other than the Federal Reserve.

All of these people leverage the position of economist to get work done, but comparing the data related to these positions across companies to identify trends would be a worthless endeavor. If an investor were to try to understand workforce trends or even company trends from changes in these positions, any conclusion that would be drawn would be inexplicable or counterintuitive. An investor may look at my team of economists and say we are overinvesting in research, without understanding that this economist team has a direct influence on our clients' happiness (by helping them understand our data) and on gaining new clients (by supporting our marketing efforts).

I understand the nuance between the economist roles across IBM, Amazon, and my company, but that's because I have direct, qualitative experience in how those companies operate. I have acquired that knowledge through many conversations—and through direct experience at IBM and my own company. Very few people have that kind of understanding of how different companies' workforces are arranged and leveraged.

Workforce taxonomies offer this kind of standardized information to anyone. With appropriately designed taxonomies, we can give more accurate titles to positions or have a deeper understanding of what a position title means. We can see if a company is hiring a macroeconomist who specializes in forecasting or a microeconomist who will help with client success. We can say with high levels of certainty that two jobs are indeed alike, across companies or even industries, and make analyses based on those comparisons. We can do this because the job titles are not based on arbitrary labels but are systematically determined and categorized through a robust data analysis process. They are developed through a combination of activities, which are the essential building blocks of work.

With these taxonomies accessible, investors can make strong inferences about the behavior and health of companies and invest accordingly. For example, if a corporation makes a big announcement about investing in one area—like AI or VR—with the goal of becoming a market leader, we can look at the workforce data to understand how committed the corporation is to this investment. If company data show that the salary it is looking to pay for engineers with an AI or VR specialty is way below market rate, you know that it is not going to obtain the top talent to execute on its bold vision. An investor interested in AI or VR might not want to put too much time or money into a company that isn't serious about its commitment.

Key Data for Investors

What is the most important data investors can pull from taxonomies?

Data can cover a variety of areas, not just hiring and firing. If an investor wants to capture a true picture of the health of a company, then the firm should consider not just the total headcount but also breakdown of the teams, and even get more granular. The investor can look not just at the overall sales team or engineering team or admin team but at what type of engineers are being hired with what types of skills. If the engineer is being hired to support AI product development—what kind of AI? If it's a blockchain engineer, what does that mean? Why does this company need so many economists? More granular data can support more nuanced understanding of company operations.

In our experience at Revelio, investors should be looking at four key pieces of data: employee profiles, job postings, employee perception, and salary benchmarks.

Employee Profiles

The most foundational thing you can know about a company is the stock and flow of its employees. These elements take into account three things: count, inflow, and outflow, meaning the total number of employees, the number of people leaving, and the number of people coming in. The data can be analyzed at the company level, each month, and offer investors aggregate headcounts, hiring rates, and attrition rates. The data can also be disaggregated by all sorts of employee characteristics within the taxonomy, such as occupation, seniority, skill, or activity.

If investors find that there is a spike in attrition rate of salespeople in a company, for example, this is probably not a good sign. The data are signaling that the company is either struggling to make sales, so salespeople are leaving en masse, or the company culture is hostile to sales. Either way, sales are going to go down, which will have a direct impact on company performance and profit.

Another red flag might be if accountants and auditors begin to quit en masse. The departure of people in these professions may indicate that some level of fraud is going on. The people who are in charge of keeping fraud from happening do not want to work at the company anymore, either because their work isn't being respected or they are being pushed out to allow the fraud to continue.

Job Postings

Job postings—basically, the company's intent to hire—can also provide useful information. Barclays, through its equity research team, analyzed a joint venture between two companies. One company essentially provided specialized services for another company through a long-standing partnership. The joint venture was up for renewal in a few months, but it became clear to Barclays that the company receiving the services was not going to extend the partnership. How did Barclays know? Because that company had started to hire employees who would fill the function of the joint venture inside the company rather than having to contract the work out. Why would the company do this if it wanted to extend the partnership? It wouldn't, and it didn't: The joint venture was canceled. That kind of information is helpful for investors to know and understand the landscape of their investments or potential portfolio companies.

Employee Perception

Employees have a very good sense of how a company is performing or will perform. After all, they are the core engine of a company. They have access to specialized knowledge that no one else has. Employee perception—essentially, how employees feel about where they work—can tell investors a lot about how a company functions.

Employee dissatisfaction with things could mean things aren't going well for the direction of the company. If employees disapprove of leadership, they might have performance concerns about the CEO, or a potential leadership turnover might be coming. Employee satisfaction with a recent acquisition could be an indication that there will be better integration (and maybe higher productivity) between the two newly merged teams.

Employee perception also relates to company culture. A worse company culture will drive attrition, which will increase the company's costs to rehire and generally get work done. If the company has a toxic culture, then it will be much harder to hire people in the roles the company needs. If there's no confidence in the CEO, for example, or if there's the sense that this CEO is driving a toxic culture, the CEO's actions will have an impact on the culture as well as on the company bottom line.

However, the reverse of this negative employee perception is true as well: If employees love working at a company, then that company will perform at higher levels and have lower costs for hiring and keeping people employed.

In certain cases, a strong reputation can lead to several benefits beyond just lower costs and higher performance.

Companies with a strong reputation for being impressive places to work can attract the best talent—sometimes at below-market rates and with strenuous hours—because they know that once employees work this job, they will have access to almost any opportunity they would like throughout their career. McKinsey or Goldman Sachs or other industry leaders benefit from this strong reputation and employee perception.

This reputational benefit occurs in all corners of our economy, including entertainment. For example, the comedian and actor James Austin Johnson has discussed how he was offered a job at the late-night program *Saturday Night Live* at the worst time in his life to get such a job offer : His wife was pregnant and they had just set up their house in Los Angeles. Taking the job would have forced them to move across the country, and the first few years on the show are known for being particularly brutal in terms of work expectations and lower pay.

However, Johnson took the job. I think anyone would have. He did so because he knew that if he worked on *SNL*, he would have the ability to provide for his family for life. Being associated with the show—even for just one season—was such a boost to his career that he knew he could coast on that reputation for as long as he needed to. He has since been promoted to full cast member and has been in some high-profile movies. The decision certainly worked out for him.

I can't imagine many investors are putting their money into NBC based on the reputation of one show, but employee sentiment of a company is hard data that is predictive of performance. By using employee sentiment to guide investment decisions, investors can make smarter choices about high-performing companies.

Salary Benchmarks

When we talk to investors about potentially investing in Revelio, one thing we share with them is our employee salaries. One thing we always hear in response is: Wow, you pay a lot.

Some investors question this strategy. They ask us why we have chosen to pay so much above market rates. They think we are throwing money away.

But the reality is that we have a different talent strategy from other companies. We are not paying our employees with artificially high salaries. Instead, we have made an intentional choice to set higher salaries because we have high standards for our employees. If they can't meet our standards, we let them go.

If someone works at Revelio, we consider them a part of an elite team. We treat them accordingly, including with high compensation. We give people raises before they ask because we want to make sure their compensation accurately reflects their work, not whether they thought to for a raise. This strategy actually is pretty cost-effective for us.

Here's an example of how we've actually saved money by paying higher salaries: We spend a bit under $1 million a year on our web scraping team. This team pulls all the data from the internet to train our model. Many companies have such teams composed of armies of low-cost employees (often offshore, where standards are lower), but most companies spend much more on the process—millions a year.

How can we keep our costs so low? Because we employ a few engineers to design and manage a program that has automated this process for us. With a "dense" team of fewer people, we also have fewer coordination costs. We don't need to hire a project manager or any other sort of middle manager. Coordination between teams is also cheaper because each employee is more familiar with a larger scope of the project.

Other companies ship their web scraping process overseas and hire many, many engineers, with a lower cost of living and therefore lower salaries—maybe the equivalent of $12,000 a year. Of course, these companies need many more of these engineers because they have lower levels of education and experience. It's also harder to manage offshore resources. All things considered, it requires more employees to do the same thing our engineers can do with a much smaller team.

If investors were to compare Revelio salaries for our engineers to the company that was spending $4 million on a larger team, they might come away believing that we are crazy for paying so much money for something we could get much cheaper. But the truth is that these are different jobs. The offshore engineers are doing much lower-skilled tasks than what our engineers are doing. It's not an apples-to-apples comparison.

Salary benchmarks can and should be an important part of investor data, but only if we can have standards to appropriately compare similar jobs. Without those standards, developed through taxonomies, the comparisons are practically worthless. It would be a valid concern if a company is overpaying employees, because that could signal that the company was not efficient or not ready to scale.

Comparisons Across Companies

As with all things related to workforce data, standards and comparisons are critical. Investors should not look at just a single company's data when making their assessments. Looking at the data from only a single company could miss broader market moves.

Consider the company that is losing all kinds of salespeople. That could be a big red flag, unless it's happening everywhere, or at least everywhere in an industry. Maybe sales are down across the board, which could mean that a slowdown in spending is affecting everything.

Without knowing, however, what is being compared, these data will be meaningless. Investors are stuck in a Tower of Babel situation, not knowing what the data are saying to each other. They cannot identify the signal from the noise.

With taxonomies, all of these comparisons become standardized and useful. Investors can make appropriate comparisons and informed decisions about the best use of their capital, based on the true engine of a company: its people.

Next I continue our exploration of the benefits of taxonomies by sharing how HR professionals and other leaders can leverage taxonomies for organizational success.

10

How Taxonomies Enable Organizational Success

We saw in Chapter 9 that investors can use taxonomies to diagnose or understand problems or challenges within a company. HR managers are the flip side of this equation: They use taxonomies to understand and execute on the treatment. If an investor sees that a company is underinvesting in its sales team, for example, then the HR team can use the data collected and analyzed through taxonomies to execute on how to fill this gap and strengthen the company.

Taxonomies can be—and in many places, already are—a part of every single HR project within a firm. Anything that involves human resources requires taxonomies. Because a company is nothing without its people, anything a company does will require a deliberate and robust analysis of its people. Any analysis of people will require segmentation and breaking a workforce into groups, which requires some level of categorization and labeling, which is another way to say taxonomies. Taxonomies should not just be relevant for HR but for sales, products, marketing, or any other function within the firm. Everyone within a company should be concerned about analyzing people and, therefore, should be concerned about taxonomies.

All management is fundamentally work transformation. When there is an issue within a team or a new directive from company leadership, the only way to respond is by having employees do more of one activity and less of another. If a sales target is missed or a competitor starts to take up more market share, managers need to respond by changing the nature of the work and the work of their teams. These management decisions can be made using qualitative information or other more instinctive decision-making, or these decisions can be more quantitative and data driven. We can't transform work successfully without workforce data and the taxonomies that help us organize that information.

Taxonomies have tremendous implications for any firm, company, or organization, regardless of size, scope, or industry. The benefits of taxonomies primarily accrue to the HR function, but the implications of a robust and established taxonomy for workforce intelligence within a company can support almost every element of decision-making. Such a taxonomy can help individual managers scope work between teams through the transformation of activities, but it can also support the management between people and teams through workforce strategy projects, in which a company considers a long-term outlook and decides what occupations it should invest in for the next phase of company growth.

Whenever people must be managed, taxonomies are necessary. This chapter outlines how leaders can leverage taxonomies to support better management of their organizations, starting with a case study from my time at IBM and then moving into practical advice for different areas within a firm.

IBM Case Study: How Poor Taxonomies Stymie Workforce Strategic Planning

One of my biggest projects at IBM was supporting its internal consulting business to help it create a strategic plan for building out its workforce. The consulting side of the business was around 100,000 people, so the team was quite large, and very dependent on human capital. Our consultants offered clients support with all different types of technology implementation projects, such as integrating new software, creating internal company apps, and troubleshooting some software issue. If the consulting side of the business were to succeed, it needed to understand the market for consulting projects and what types of roles, skills, and occupations were needed to meet the demand from potential clients.

To understand what skills we had in-house, each member of the consulting team was tagged with a specific job category. This was, essentially, the basic workforce taxonomy within IBM. An internal team manually created and maintained this taxonomy. My job category, at the time, would have been something like strategy consultant—data science. Each of these categories would have a numerical value that allowed them to be analyzed. There were thousands of categories, and we could manipulate the data to better understand the sum total of the skills IBM had to offer its clients.

We were tasked with determining which occupations were in demand and which were not. My people analytics team did this by tracking requests for proposals or other in-bound client needs and aggregating those requests to see the total demand. We also considered the salaries of positions that would be required to meet this demand, to understand what resources IBM would need to dedicate to any recommendations we offered. Through the existing taxonomy, as basic as it was, we were able to match the existing "supply" of services through our consulting workforce with the "demand" of potential projects that clients wanted.

Through our analysis, we were able to find which occupations we had overinvested in and which we had underinvested in. There were some job categories where we had a lot of people, but there was little demand. There were other job categories with a ton of demand, but we did not have enough people employed to meet that demand. Once we fully understood which projects were in demand, we could make recommendations on how the consulting division could better strategically plan to build out its workforce.

For example, we had a large team of software engineers who were experts in a programming language called COBOL. This programming language was once very much in demand and was used to program ATMs. IBM, at one point, was very successful in helping clients build out and implement COBOL software.

But as times changed, programming languages changed. By the early 2000s, very few companies were looking to hire consultants who had experience with COBOL. We were able to take an analytical and strategic view of the data to recommend that it was highly unlikely that IBM would receive enough inbound requests for COBOL projects to warrant maintaining a COBOL team.

My team and I worked hard on this project. Although the project may seem simple, offering those kinds of recommendations at scale—remember, we were analyzing about 100,000 jobs—was complex and high stakes. The project had a tremendous amount of visibility in the company, because we were taking an analytical approach to IBM's workforce in a way that hadn't been done before.

Although we produced sound recommendations based on our data analysis, unfortunately, the implementation of those recommendations did not go over as we had hoped. We were limited in what we could do by the existing taxonomies within the company. Because we were relying on a very basic understanding of how jobs were categorized through the existing system, we were not able to give the nuanced advice a project like this required.

First, the data we had about the workforce were poorly categorized. We ended up with a lot of nonsensical job categorizations that clearly were a result of poor data categorization and poor maintenance. Some job categories were misspelled (like "Jaav" instead of "Java") or misaligned across teams (a software engineer on one team was a product manager on another). This problem led to many outliers in our data at the end of the spectrum, forcing us to spend a lot of time understanding what the data were telling us. There was no regular routine of data cleaning to fix these issues or understanding of the work being done across teams, and at the scale of 100,000 jobs, it would have been impossible to offer solid recommendations using this less-than-perfect data.

On top of this issue with data collection and maintenance, there was also an issue about modeling the demand for the different skills. We understood the demand for projects based on the requests that project leads submitted, but often these requests were miscategorized and nonstandardized, just like the job category taxonomy. If a project was requested as a premium service (meaning higher paying), for example, it would have been listed at higher demand, but that didn't mean that there were necessarily a lot of requests for that particular project, requiring more employees with that job category. At the time, an AI project would have been a very rare request, given the newness of the technology, but if it was requested, it would have been offered at a premium price. This finding could have signified many different things: that IBM should not have built out an AI practice, given how few AI-related projects there were. Or IBM could have come to an opposite conclusion: There was growing demand for AI, and at a high premium, and the company should get ahead of the trend and invest in a workforce that could handle AI projects.

Besides the mismatch of both supply and demand, there was a breakdown in implementation after we made our recommendations. This breakdown was related to one fundamental problem with the existing taxonomy system: It said nothing about a person's productivity. When we recommended that certain employees switch teams, their managers would resist, because sometimes those people were the highest performers on their teams. The job categories could tell us nothing about the work being done by specific employees, so our recommendations said nothing about the overall productivity of the team. Maybe that COBOL software engineer was serving more as a project manager within the team and completed very little specific activities related to a programming language. Transferring this engineer away from the team might have reduced overall productivity, and therefore cost IBM money, while we were trying to do the exact opposite.

If IBM had a solid taxonomy at the time, we could have approached this project quite differently. Better understanding the work activities that potential clients were looking to complete would have offered a more standardized and grounded way to forecast both demand and supply. We still might have come up with the same recommendations—more Java, less COBOL, in the specific case of that team—but we would have been able to offer more nuanced guidance to the entire consulting function.

For example, we could have helped teams and managers shift people on their teams to other teams that had higher needs. Through this project, we were essentially telling managers: "I see you have 10 people here, but we are projecting demand for only 5. This other team has 10 people, but they need 15. So we are giving 5 of your team to this other team." If you have ever dealt with a restructuring, you can see why this recommendation did not go over well. Managers will hold on to their people as tightly as they can, because team size can be very much tied to managers' overall influence within a company.

Instead, if we were able to understand the work activities that needed to be completed, we could have said: "I see you are only doing the work of 5 people, and so we are going to assign you more work activities to be completed. This other team is doing the work of 15 people but only has 10, so you will be taking on some of their tasks." This approach would have spread out the work being completed more evenly and also allowed the consulting teams to be nimbler and more responsive to the demands of potential clients.

How Taxonomies Can Benefit Organizational Leaders

My experience at IBM illustrates just one way in which a better taxonomy would have supported better firm decision-making. This was an example specifically in the area of workforce training or professional development. But taxonomies can offer benefits to firms in every area of their human resources function.

This section lays out the takeaways for organizational leaders (specifically those within HR) and how taxonomies can support them in better management of their employees and operational decision-making. Many of these themes or recommendations have been touched on previously, so I will not go into each in depth. Instead, this section serves more as a checklist or a comprehensive place for all the reasons firms can benefit from taxonomies.

Talent Acquisition

With taxonomies, firms can source candidates with more clarity and using the language that job candidates understand. Taxonomies will help hiring managers align job postings with how job seekers are presenting themselves, reducing inefficiencies in the hiring process. This benefit is related to Chapter 8 on job seekers, in which I walked through how taxonomies can break down silos and jargon between employers and their future employees.

Talent Intelligence

Talent intelligence, like talent acquisition, benefits from the clarity that taxonomies offer. Whereas talent acquisition is concerned with bringing in individual candidates, talent intelligence can use taxonomies to select the markets with the best talent pools for a company. Taxonomies offer more visibility in the market sourcing process, supporting an understanding of cross-sectional differences between different markets and geographies.

For example, if Amazon wants to open a new distribution site, it can use taxonomies to understand which geography has the most optimal workforce mix of potential employees. If a company needs to find a market with a lot of people who are skilled in mechanical engineering, for example, taxonomies can help it understand which skills are related to mechanical engineering and then which geographies have the total mix of all the relevant skills.

Compensation Benchmarking and Employee Experience

Robust benchmarking of any employee compensation is almost impossible without taxonomies. It's not enough to look just at the titles of occupations and compare them across companies, because it's highly unlikely that occupations with the same name at two different companies are the same job. Through taxonomies, companies can better understand the work being done within their jobs and compare like to like and then understand how competitors are compensating the same work being done in their own companies. A better understanding of compensation can help companies become more competitive and attract the best talent.

Compensation is not the only priority for employees. Taxonomies can help companies understand and compare the total value proposition they are offering to potential employees, including benefits, commute time, and more intangible things like work-life balance.

Pay Equity

Related to compensation benchmarking and employee experience, taxonomies support an understanding of pay equity. With a benchmark in place, taxonomies can support understanding if there are any disparities, internally or externally, in terms of compensation for certain demographic groups. For example, taxonomies can show if women are being paid less than men for the same work or if certain subgroups are being promoted at different rates.

Taxonomies also help solve for a common flaw in pay equity recommendations: They control for seniority without meaning to. Often, and this is the case with using O*NET, pay equity analyses do not separate out seniority and occupation. When looking at the difference in pay between men and women, you may find there is no disparity. That is likely because disparities are a problem only within roles—meaning that if there is a pay disparity between a senior manager or a manager, that isn't a problem because we would expect someone with higher seniority to make more than someone with lower seniority. But unless you look at how many women actually are being promoted into senior roles, you will ignore the disparities that may exist. It may be that men are being promoted into senior roles at much higher rates than women, and so therefore a pay disparity does exist. Many taxonomies conflate seniority with occupations and make separate categories for senior manager and manager. Without a robust taxonomy that carefully distinguishes between occupation and seniority, there would be no way to understand existing inequities in pay.

People Analytics

A people analytics department spends its days analyzing groups of employees to make recommendations to leadership on how best to use its workforce. This is what I was doing at IBM, and without robust taxonomies, we had a very difficult time doing our jobs. Taxonomies help make the internal comparisons between teams possible, just as they make benchmarking between companies possible. Without a standardized understanding of the work being done, people analytics departments will struggle to make recommendations with any fidelity. Taxonomies can support stronger analyses based on clear and robust segmentations of employees.

Strategic Workforce Planning

The function of strategic workforce planning is a cousin to the work of people analytics. Strategic workforce planning is more about the broader trends within the workforce and how to project a future workforce on future company needs: Do we have the employees we need? Where are the gaps? Where do we have too much of an employee type?

With taxonomies, strategic workforce planning departments can understand how a company compares to competitors and what positions are needed to remain competitive with competitors. Taxonomies, with their detailed breakdown of skills and activities being completed by which employees, can help strategic workforce teams understand which of these roles can be filled in house and which need to be hired for. Should those positions be part time, full time, or contract? By using the taxonomy to get a full scope of the company, the strategic workforce team can engage with other departments—such as hiring, procurement, or people analytics—to create a unified, forward-looking vision for the company and its workforce.

Organizational Design

Taxonomies can help in constructing an organizational chart. Because they break down who completes what work, taxonomies can help to build an org chart and management structure based on the nature of work. Once the activities of the work are understood, then the company leaders can have a conversation about which aspects of the work have dependencies to each other and, therefore, how the work should be structured or managed.

Instead of having a team of only front-end engineers, separate from back-end engineers or middleware engineers, it may make more sense to have several, smaller teams of all three of these kinds of employees, managed by someone who oversees the entire project management process. Because all their work is so dependent on each other, siloing them based on occupation, rather than on work activities, would create inefficiencies. A more comprehensive look at the work being done will allow for more seamless operation.

In this way, taxonomies can help a company create a more forward-looking design of its workflow. Instead of relying on rigid org charts, taxonomies allow a deeper analysis and understanding of what exactly is being completed and allow management to adapt to that workflow rather than forcing the workflow into a predetermined organizational structure.

M&A Integration

The process of merger and acquisition (M&A) integration is an extreme example of organizational design. When two companies come together, they are essentially creating a new organization from two existing ones. Doing that can cause many challenges, as each has its own long-established ways of doing things.

Taxonomies can help the two firms understand how they should best work together. Because of the comparability of work across the companies, leaders can determine exactly what work needs to get done, and where. Teams can be created or merged using a deeper understanding of what exactly the employees are doing rather than relying on job titles that may seemingly match but in fact do not. Because taxonomies break down the fundamental building blocks of the work being done, leaders can use them to build back up a new organization that functions just as well, if not better, than the old ones.

Conclusion: Putting Job Architecture to Work—Everywhere

SO MANY OF our problems are driven by the way we have structured our labor markets. People are stuck in jobs they are not well suited for, limiting their overall productivity. Being trapped in a job they do not like makes them less useful members of society and, ultimately, forces many to not reach their full potential.

These inefficiencies have a tremendous impact on the way our firms operate. They are unable to find the people they need for the work that needs to get done. Managers are forced to spend unnecessary time on coordination, usually in seemingly endless meetings, to determine the most effective use of their team's time. There is no way to manage a team with clarity and rigor.

The introduction of this book described how—when it comes to the most important decisions for an organization—we are flying blind. Increasingly, our economy is becoming more reliant on services and human capital and less on physical capital, but we do not have the necessary data infrastructure to support this shift. We make decisions about labor markets with little more than instinct and gut feel, whereas the financial markets can use precise, standardized, and robust data to determine the most efficient and productive ways to deploy capital.

Much of the revolution in analytics for capital markets occurred in the last 70 years. In just a few decades, Wall Street traders went from relying on spurious reports and insider tips to guide their investment decisions to the widespread adoption of Bloomberg Terminals.

We are in the midst of a similar shift within labor markets. Powerful workforce intelligence technologies—driven by tools for processing big datasets—allow us to segment and properly analyze labor markets and company workforces. We can translate the massive amount of information that exists online—job postings, resumes, job profiles—as well as internal company data to create powerful workforce taxonomies. These taxonomies can, in turn, power a better and deeper understanding of the way we work.

If we can make taxonomies ubiquitous, we can achieve the same level of efficiency for labor markets that we have now within capital markets. It will not be long before those in the HR function have the equivalent of the Bloomberg Terminal for human capital on their desk. They will use this information to better understand what types of employees are needed to execute on company goals and where those employees would be best positioned for success. Managers can use the information provided to them to understand how the nature of their work is changing and how to best leverage their team's talent toward their highest levels of productivity. Investors will know more about the companies they invest in and how their capital is deployed to support the growth of the company. Employees will be more fulfilled in their jobs and find better matches for work, all through a simplified application process.

Once taxonomies are everywhere, we can arrive at more solutions to problems with less process. Now, anytime companies bring in an HR tech vendor or undertake a workforce analytics project, they must undertake a costly discovery phase or build-out project. The vendor or internal team must spend a significant amount of time just understanding the nature of the company's workforce, often through the cleaning and standardizing of employee data. The work becomes understanding the problem rather than solving it. Taxonomies cut out this first half of the process or at least reduce it significantly. By using taxonomies, companies can focus on solving problems and delivering real economic benefit.

When we put job architecture to work—everywhere—we will find benefits all around us. Some possibilities follow.

Human Resources Will Become More Strategic

Right now, HR is a limited strategic partner, at best. Without the ability to analyze the workforce appropriately, HR practitioners cannot make robust and nuanced recommendations about a company's future growth opportunities. Taxonomies will help HR differentiate among employees, teams, and companies, offering a better understanding of what an individual component is doing and why and how it can be leveraged more effectively. Workforce data analysis will become cheaper and easier. Companies will save money, and HR practitioners will have fewer headaches. Benchmarking against peers and understanding a company's competitive advantage will be much simpler. HR will be able to contribute to the strategic direction of a company in a way it never has before.

Management Will Become Smarter

Right now managers have little, if any, quantitative data to understand how their teams should be assembled and managed. As work changes and transforms, the task of management becomes even harder. Taxonomies will offer a clear picture to management of what exact work activities are needed to fulfill company goals or milestones and how to best complete those tasks by managing those employees. Management will focus more intentionally on the work of managing transformation, reacting to employee needs, or responding to directives from company leadership, with precision and rigor. Employee preferences are always shifting, staff come and go, and business strategies shift. When work changes, as it always does, managers can take stock of what work is being done, who's doing it, and how they can adapt to a new set of work requirements or constraints. This process of management will become easier, more sophisticated, and better structured.

Transparency Will Increase and Friction Will Be Reduced

Taxonomies offer a more useful unit of analysis for human capital analysis and indicators than our current status quo.

When data are presented more cleanly, analysis becomes easier and recommendations become more transparent. A company's pay, benefits, attrition rates, and more will be easily available for anyone to see and understand, helping to create a level playing field for hiring managers and job seekers alike.

This transparency will also lead to a better understanding of the work required within a job and therefore to better matches between employees and employers. The complicated process that is hiring will be significantly streamlined, reducing overall friction in the labor market and leading to efficiencies that accrue to everyone: employers, employees, and shareholders.

Companies Will Be Evaluated More Effectively

More transparency and cleaner data support a standardization of workforce data across companies. This standardization, in turn, means better comparison opportunities between companies. Investors will be able to get a fuller picture of what is happening under a company's roof and better allocate their capital, given that information. Finance will become less of a zero-sum game and more about directing capital to where a potential return is most probable—leading to a more efficient economy.

We Will Lead More Fulfilling Lives

All of this improved efficiency ultimately leads to one thing: more fulfilling lives. People find themselves in jobs they enjoy and are better suited for. They have a better understanding of the work that needs to get done and therefore can be more productive. They spend less time doing things they do not want to do, or do not need to do, and more time doing what they care about and are good at.

A boost in productivity and more fulfillment through work affects everything around us. We will have greater economic growth and a more productive economy. Taxonomies can unlock all of this for us, if we let them.

We are at the early stages of an emerging science for workforce intelligence, which will lead to a world in which human capital can be analyzed rigorously and in a standard way. Changes in technology are driving this science, but, ultimately, it will be up to us to adopt what the taxonomies are offering us and put them to work. If we can harness the power of taxonomies, there is no limit to how we can transform the way we work and how we run our companies.

Notes

Introduction

1. Carol Deeb, "Percent of a Business Budget for Salary," CHRON, n.d. https://smallbusiness.chron.com/percent-business-budget-salary-14254.html
2. Indeed Employer Content Team, "What Is the Cost of Hiring New Employees," *Indeed for Employers*, January 28, 2025. www.indeed.com/hire/c/info/cost-of-hiring-employees
3. Stuart Banner, "The Origin of the New York Stock Exchange, 1791–1860," *Journal of Legal Studies* 27, no. 1 (1998): 113–140. www.jstor.org/stable/10.1086/468015
4. John Kay, "Enduring Lessons from the Legend of Rothschild's Carrier Pigeon," *Financial Times*, May 28, 2013. www.ft.com/content/255b75e0-c77d-11e2-be27-00144feab7de

Chapter 2

1. L. Bock, *Work Rules!: Insights from Inside Google that Will Transform How You Live and Lead*. Grand Central Publishing, 2015.

2. GAO, *Sole Proprietor Compliance: Treasury and IRS Have Opportunities to Reduce the Tax Gap*. GAO-24-105281, October 19, 2023. www.gao.gov/products/gao-24-105281
3. Alex Hern, "The Two-Pizza Rule and the Secret of Amazon's Success," *The Guardian*, April 24, 2018. www.theguardian.com/technology/2018/apr/24/the-two-pizza-rule-and-the-secret-ofamazons-success
4. Jeff Hader, "When Jeff Bezos's 2-Pizza Teams Fell Short, He Turned to the Brilliant Model Amazon Uses Today," *Inc.*, February 18, 2021. www.inc.com/jeff-haden/when-jeff-bezoss-two-pizza-teams-fell-short-he-turned-to-brilliant-model-amazon-uses-today.html
5. Claudia Golden, *Career and Family: Women's Century-Long Journey toward Equity*, Princeton University Press, 2021.

Chapter 3

1. Peter Dizikes, "Most Work Is New Work, Long-Term Study of U.S. Census Data Shows," *MIT News*, April 1, 2024. https://news.mit.edu/2024/most-work-is-new-work-us-census-data-shows-0401
2. James Pethokoukis, "What the Story of ATMs and Bank Tellers Reveals About the 'Rise of the Robots' and Jobs," *AEIdeas* [blog], June 6, 2016. www.aei.org/economics/what-atms-bank-tellers-rise-robots-and-jobs/
3. Martha C. White, "Small Businesses Who Pivoted to Make Masks and Sanitizer Are Still Feeling the Hit to Their Bottom Line," NBC News, September 22, 2021. www.nbcnews.com/business/business-news/small-businesses-who-pivoted-make-masks-sanitizer-are-still-feeling-n1279767
4. *Forbes Quotes*, General George S. Patton, www.forbes.com/quotes/3327/

Chapter 4

1. David Deming, "In Defense of Email Jobs," *Forked Lightning* [blog], October 15, 2024. https://forklightning.substack.com/p/in-defense-of-email-jobs; see also James Feigenbaum and

Daniel P. Gross, "Answering the Call of Automation: How the Labor Market Adjusted to Mechanizing Telephone Operation," *Quarterly Journal of Economics* 139, no. 3 (2024): 1879–1939. https://doi.org/10.1093/qje/qjae005

Chapter 5

1. Kunal Handa, Alex Tamkin, Miles McCain, Saffron Huang . . . Deep Ganguli, "Which Economic Tasks Are Performed with AI? Evidence from Millions of Claude Conversations," arXiv preprint, arXiv:2503.04761 (2025). https://doi.org/10.48550/arXiv.2503.04761

Chapter 7

1. Marc Effron, "Is the Juice Worth the Squeeze? Questions About Becoming a Skills-based Organization," Talent Strategy Group, February 12, 2024. https://talentstrategygroup.com/is-the-juice-worth-the-squeeze/
2. Shrihari Vasudevan, Moninder Singh, Joydeep Mondal, Michael Peran, Benjamin Zweig, Brian Johnston, and Rachel Rosenfeld, "Estimating Fungibility Between Skills by Combining Skill Similarities Obtained from Multiple Data Sources," *Data Science and Engineering* 3 (2018): 248–262. https://doi.org/10.1007/s41019-018-0075-3

Chapter 8

1. Krista Soria and Mark Bultmann, "Supporting Working-Class Students in Higher Education," *NACADA Journal* 34, no. 2 (2014): 51–62. doi:https://doi.org/10.12930/NACADA-13-017; Emily Forrest Cataldi, Christopher T. Bennett, and Xianglei Chen, "First-Generation Students: College Access, Persistence, and Postbachelor's Outcomes," National Center for Education Statistics Report (February 2018), NCES 20184 21.https://nces.ed.gov/use-work/resource-library/report/statistics-brief/first-generation-students-college-access-persistence-and-postbachelors-outcomes?pubid=2018421; Kate H. Choi, R.

Kelly Raley, Chandra Muller, and Catherine Riegle-Crumb, "A Longitudinal Analysis of Contextual Exposure to Peers with College Educated Parents and Students' College Enrollment," *Social Science Quarterly* 89, no. 4 (2008): 846–866. doi: https://doi.org/10.1111/j.1540-6237.2008.00587.x; James Tompsett and Chris Knoestr, "Family Socioeconomic Status and College Attendance: A Consideration of Individual-Level and School-Level Pathways," *PLoSOne* 18, no. 4 (2023). doi: https://doi.org/10.1371/journal.pone.0284188.
2. Katie Navarra, "The Real Costs of Recruitment," *SHRM Online*, April 11, 2022. www.shrm.org/topics-tools/news/talent-acquisition/real-costs-recruitment
3. Stephanie Hao and Lisa K. Simon, "Ghost Job Postings," Revelio Labs Macro, October 31, 2023, www.reveliolabs.com/news/macro/ghost-job-postings/

Chapter 9

1. Ben Werschkul, "It's Lonely in the Metaverse: Decentraland's 38 Daily Active Users in a $1.3B Ecosystem," Yahoo Finance, October 6, 2022. www.finance.yahoo.com/news/lonely-metaverse-decentraland-38-daily-172132354.html
2. Matthew Boyle, "Metaverse Jobs Are Disappearing as Hiring Slows at Google, Facebook," Bloomberg, July 28, 2022. www.bloomberg.com/news/articles/2022-07-29/metaverse-jobs-are-disappearing-as-hiring-slows-at-google-facebook

Acknowledgments

THIS BOOK WOULDN'T exist without the brilliant team of data scientists at Revelio Labs that I've been lucky to work with—especially Daniel Firester and Bruce Langford—who brought their creativity, persistence, and good humor to the many versions of the taxonomies we built together. I'm also grateful to Lisa Simon, our chief economist, for being a thoughtful sounding board along the way.

I've learned a lot over the years from scholars like John Boudreau and Daniel Rock, whose work helped shape the ideas in these pages.

Special thanks to my cofounder, Yedidya Gorsetman, for building this journey with me from the beginning—and for being the rare kind of partner who makes the hard parts easier and the fun parts more fun.

And finally, to Ariel, Emmy, and Nava—thank you for your love, your patience, and your willingness to let me pontificate about jobs and work for longer than anyone should.

About the Author

BEN ZWEIG IS a labor economist and the CEO of Revelio Labs, a workforce intelligence company.

A passionate advocate for understanding the evolving nature of work, Ben also teaches a course titled "The Future of Work" at NYU Stern. Before founding Revelio Labs, he was a managing data scientist at IBM's Chief Analytics Office and a quantitative strategist at an emerging markets hedge fund. He holds a PhD in Economics from the CUNY Graduate Center, where his research explored occupational transformation and social mobility.

Ben combines academic insight, industry experience, and a frontline view of workforce trends to offer a sharp perspective in job architecture. His work lies at the intersection of economics, technology, and workforce strategy, establishing him as an authoritative voice on the future of labor.

Index

ability to evolve, 116, 124–125
Accenture, 144
Acemoglu, Daron, 67
activity-based approach, 117
activity taxonomies, 104, 106–108
adaptability, 70, 116
  in taxonomies, 119–121
  work, 75–78
agile methodology, 52–53
AI. *See* artificial intelligence (AI)
Amazon
  Amazon Web Services (AWS), 40
  bundling and categorization, 38–40
  economists hiring, 149
ambitious employees, 55
applying for jobs, 136–137
architecture, of work, 17–19

capital markets standardization, 24–26
elements of work, 22–24
engineer and his stopwatch, 20–22, 33, 53, 63
everywhere, 173–175
labor markets standardization, 26–28
artificial intelligence (AI), 28, 36, 61
  adoption of, 74–75
  case study, 73–74
assembly line, 66
AT&T, 72
auditability, 116, 121–123
automated teller machines (ATMs), 50
automation, 36, 61, 70, 73

backward compatibility, 99
banking, 50–51

188 INDEX

Barclays, 152
Bezos, Jeff, 39
blockchain, 117
Bloomberg Terminals, 11, 127, 174
Bock, Laszlo, 36
"bottom-up" transformation, 54–55
breaking down, of tasks, 21
budget, operating, 8
bundled work, 32–33
   and categorization, 37–38
   common skills and interests, 42–43
   hiring cost, 43–44
   information sharing, 44–45
   within same process, 40–42
   shared language, 45–46
business intelligence (BI) engineer, 138
business policy, 148–149
business process changes, 63
Buttonwood Agreement, 9

capital
   disclosures, 147
   and labor, 6–9
   production, 28
capital markets, 24–26, 127, 174
career development, 137–138, 140
carrier pigeons, 10
categorization, 37–38, 49, 83, 109
   activity, 106–108
   and bundling work, 37–38
   role (occupation), 108–111
   skill, 111–114
ChatGPT, 74, 94, 98
cloud computing, 68

clustering, 88–92, 106, 109–111
Coase, Ronald, 32–33
COBOL software, 163–165
command-and-control structure, 39
common skills and interests, 42–43
compensation, 167–168
coordination costs, 35
COVID-19 pandemic, 52, 64
crypto exchange FTX, 142–143

data collection, 85–86, 106
data science, 124–125
decision making, 6, 10, 134
Deep Blue computer, 73
Deming, David, 71–72
demographic changes, 63
depreciation, 25
Dictionary of Occupational Titles (DOT), 26–27
dimensionality, 98
disruptions, work, 62–64

economists, 148
electric engine, 65
electricity, 67
embeddings, 84, 86–88, 108
employee(s)
   ambitious, 55
   compensation, 167–168
   perception, 153–154
   profiles, 151–152
   retention, 2–3, 19
   sentiment, 154
   See also job seekers, and employees

employment shifts, 13
Enron scandal, 63
entrepreneurship, 33
evaluation, 177

farming, 65
financial markets, 7, 9, 25
firms, value of, 32–33
flexibility, 116, 118–119, 127
forecasting, 148
freelancing, 31–32
FTX, 142–143
fulfilling lives, 177–178

Gantt, Henry, 21
generative AI, 94
generic jobs, 90
ghost jobs, 137
gigs, 31–32
Golden, Claudia, 44
Goldman Sachs, 154
greedy work, 44

hierarchies
   adaptable, 116, 119–121
   flexible, 116, 118–119
hiring cost, 43–44
human capital, 6, 8
human labor, 6, 61
human resources, 175–176

IBM, 17, 39, 123
   Deep Blue computer, 73
   people analytics, 1–2, 169
   strategic workforce planning
      case study, 161–166
   Watson, 74
in-demand jobs, 4
Industrial Revolution, 61

inferences, 95–99, 106
information lackness, 133
information sharing, 44–45
innovations, 65
internet, 62, 140
investors, 141
   company's health, 142–146
   comparisons across
      companies, 156–157
   employee perception,
      153–154
   employee profiles, 151–152
   job postings, 152
   key data for, 150–156
   salary benchmarks, 155–156
   taxonomies offer
      standards, 146–150

job(s)
   application, 136–137
   categorization, 18–19, 26, 49
   crafting, 54–55, 70
   descriptions, 19, 91
   postings, 152
   retention, 13
job seekers, and employees
   applying for jobs, 136–137
   career development,
      137–138, 140
   job transformation,
      138–139
   limiting career
      potential, 134–135
   low information
      consequences, 135–139
   taxonomies create
      standards, 139–140
   taxonomies
      supporting, 131–133

job transformation, 47, 64–69, 138–139
  acceleration of work, 49–51
  bottom-up (job crafting), 54–55
  inputs, 69
  managing, 55–58
  outputs, 66
  processes, 67–69
  tools, 67
  top-down, 51–54
John Henry (American fable), 61, 71, 77
Johnson, James Austin, 154
Just-in-Time inventory, 63–64

knowledge work, 22, 49–50

labeling, 92–95, 106
labor, and capital, 6–9
labor markets, 26–28, 174
lack of information, 133
large language model (LLM), 84, 87, 97
LDA (latent Dirichlet allocation) process, 107–108
Llama, 85
LLM. *See* large language model (LLM)
longevity, incentivize, 3
low-cost employees, 155
Luddites, 67

machine learning models, 95
management, 176
management-bound employees, 57–58
managers' role, 35–36
manual labor, 49

mappability, 116, 125–126
market structure, 149
McKinsey, 154
merger and acquisition (M&A) integration, 171
meritocracy, 135
Meta, virtual reality (VR), 143–145
micromanagement, 36
microservices, 29–30
mishiring, 18
ModernBERT, 85

natural language processing (NLP), 87
The Nature of the Firm (Coase), 32–33
Netflix, 52
networking, 133, 137
New York Stock Exchange, 9
NLP. *See* natural language processing (NLP)
nontechnological disruptions, 63

O*NET, 100, 120, 126
occupation, 24
Occupational Information Network (O*NET), 27
offshore jobs, 155–156
OpenAI, 97
operating budget, 8
orchestration, of tasks, 30–32, 35, 77
organizational design, 170–171
organizational goals, 58
organizational leaders, 159–161

compensation benchmarking
and employee
experience, 167–168
IBM case study, 161–166
M&A integration, 171
organizational design,
170–171
pay equity, 168–169
people analytics, 169
strategic workforce planning,
161–166, 169–170
talent acquisition, 166
talent intelligence, 167
organized taxonomy, 116–118
outsourcing, 31–32
overhead costs, 33

partner data integration, 85
Patton, George, 53
pay equity, 168–169
people analytics, 1–2, 169
performance, 141–142
personal computers, 59–60
Pfizer, 13
physical capital, 8
pretrained data models, 85–86
price negotiation, 31
problem solving, 131
productivity, 20, 33, 175
public data, 85

quality control, 18

regulatory changes, 63
responsibilities, 138
retention
employee, 2–3, 19
job, 13
Revelio Labs, 12–13, 81–83

role taxonomies, 104–105,
108–111
Rothschild, Nathan, 10
Rust programming, 122

salary benchmarks, 155–156,
167–168
SAP implementation, 4–5
scientific management, 21, 33
Securities and Exchange
Commission, 10, 24
self-driving vehicles, 76
shared language, 45–46
"silhouette score," 110
siloing off, work, 39
skills, 23
-based work, 43, 113–114,
116–117
and interests, common,
42–43
taxonomies, 105, 111–114
slicing process, 88–92, 104
smaller teams, 39
social media management,
41–42
sole proprietorships, 37
standardization
capital markets, 24–26
lackness in labor
markets, 26–28
of workforce data, 177
steam engine, 65
stock market, 9
strategic workforce planning,
161–166, 169–170
superworker, 37

talent acquisition, 118, 166
talent intelligence, 167

taxonomies, 78
  impact on work, 11–14
  strategic workforce planning case study, 161–166
taxonomy characteristics, 115
  ability to evolve, 116, 124–125
  adaptability, 116, 119–121
  auditability, 116, 121–123
  flexibility, 116, 118–119
  mappability, 116, 125–126
  organized, 116–118
  universality, 116, 127–128
taxonomy foundation
  clustering and slicing, 88–92
  data collection, 85–86
  embeddings and transformers, 86–88
  fundamentals, 81–84
  inferences, 95–99
  labeling, 92–95
  versioning, 99–101
Taylor, Frederick Winslow (management scientist), 20–22, 33, 53, 63
technological advancements, 60, 67
technological innovations, 65
technologies, and job transformation, 59–61, 64–66
  AI adoption, 74–75
  AI case study, 73–74
  inputs, 69
  jobs displacement, 69–71
  outputs, 66
  processes, 67–69
  telephone operators, 71–73
  tools, 67
  work adaptability, 75–78
  work disruptions, 62–64
telephone operators, 71–73, 76–77
"top-down" transformation, 51–54, 70
topic modeling, 107
Toyota, 63–64
trade-off, 121
training, 95–96
transaction costs, 39–40
transformers, 87–88, 106
transparency, 146–147, 176–177
truck driving, 76
turnover, reducing, 2–3
Twitter, 52
typewriters, 59

unbundled work, 33–35
universality, 116, 121, 125, 127–128
US, financial markets history, 9

vectors. *See* embeddings
venture capital, 10
versioning, 99–101
video conferencing, 68
virtual reality (VR), 143–145

Wall Street, 7, 10, 25, 174
wars, and technology development, 63
Watson, 74
work activities, 22–23
work disruptions, 62–64

workforce taxonomies,
    103–105, 150
  activity, 104, 106–108
  impact on, 11–14
  role, 104–105, 108–111
  skill, 105, 111–114
work, into jobs, 29–31
  Amazon and "two pizza" rule, 38–40
  bundled work, 40–46
  categorization and bundling work, 37–38
  managers role, 35–36
  Ronald Coase and The Nature of the Firm, 32–33
  unbundled work challenges, 33–35
  value of firms, 32–33
  work-on-demand approach, 31–32
Work Rules! (Bock), 36

Zuckerberg, Mark, 143–144